WeightWatchers®

Delicious recipes the whole family will love

Family Favourites

First published in Great Britain by Simon & Schuster UK Ltd, 2013
A CBS Company

Copyright © 2013, Weight Watchers International, Inc.
Simon & Schuster Illustrated Books, Simon & Schuster UK Ltd,
First Floor, 222 Gray's Inn Road, London WC1X 8HB

www.simonandschuster.co.uk

Simon & Schuster Australia, Sydney
Simon & Schuster India, New Delhi

Weight Watchers, **ProPoints** and the **ProPoints** icon are the registered
trademarks of Weight Watchers International Inc and are used under license
by Weight Watchers (UK) Ltd.

Weight Watchers Publications: Jane Griffiths, Linda Palmer and Nina McKerlie.

Recipes written by: Sue Ashworth, Sue Beveridge, Tamsin Burnett-Hall,
Cas Clarke, Siân Davies, Roz Denny, Nicola Graimes, Becky Johnson,
Kim Morphew, Joy Skipper, Penny Stephens and Wendy Veale as well
as Weight Watchers Leaders and Members.

Photography by: Iain Bagwell, Steve Baxter, Steve Lee, Juliet Piddington
and William Shaw.
Project editor: Nicki Lampon.
Design and typesetting: Martin Lampon.

Colour reproduction by Dot Gradations Ltd, UK.
Printed and bound in China.

A CIP catalogue for this book is available from the British Library

ISBN 978-1-47111-089-4

1 2 3 4 5 6 7 8 9 10

Pictured on the title page: Fish and chips p96.
Pictured on the Introduction: Roast chicken with rosemary and lemon potatoes p68,
The ultimate hash browns p16, Pear brulées p168.

Delicious recipes the whole family will love

Family Favourites

SIMON &
SCHUSTER
ILLUSTRATED

London · New York · Sydney · Toronto · New Delhi

A CBS COMPANY

Weight Watchers **ProPoints** Weight Loss System is a simple way to lose weight. As part of the Weight Watchers **ProPoints** plan you'll enjoy eating delicious, healthy, filling foods that help to keep you feeling satisfied for longer and in control of your portions.

Ⓥ This symbol denotes a vegetarian recipe and assumes that, where relevant, free range eggs, vegetarian cheese, vegetarian virtually fat free fromage frais, vegetarian low fat crème fraîche and vegetarian low fat yogurts are used. Virtually fat free fromage frais, low fat crème fraîche and low fat yogurts may contain traces of gelatine so they are not always vegetarian. Please check the labels.

❄ This symbol denotes a dish that can be frozen. Unless otherwise stated, you can freeze the finished dish for up to 3 months. Defrost thoroughly and reheat until the dish is piping hot throughout.

Recipe notes

Egg size: Medium sized, unless otherwise stated.

Raw eggs: Only the freshest eggs should be used. Pregnant women, the elderly and children should avoid recipes with eggs that are not fully cooked or raw.

All fruits and vegetables: Medium sized, unless otherwise stated.

Stock: Stock cubes are used in recipes, unless otherwise stated. These should be prepared according to packet instructions.

Recipe timings: These are approximate and meant to be guidelines. Please note that the preparation time includes all the steps up to and following the main cooking time(s).

Microwaves: Timings and temperatures are for a standard 800 W microwave. If necessary, adjust your own microwave.

Low fat spread: Where a recipe states to use a low fat spread, a light spread with a fat content of no less than 38% should be used.

Low fat soft cheese: Where low fat soft cheese is specified in a recipe, this refers to soft cheese with a fat content of less than 5%.

Contents

Introduction   7

Brunches and lunches   12

Marvellous meat   40

Perfect poultry   66

Fantastic fish and seafood   94

Simply vegetarian   120

Delicious desserts   146

Index   172

Introduction

Everyone wants their family to eat healthy, delicious meals, but recipes that the whole family love can sometimes be difficult to find. This wonderful collection from the best of Weight Watchers cookbooks is here to save the day – it's packed full of tasty *Family Favourites* that everyone will really enjoy.

Try Eggy Crumpets 'n' Bacon for a weekend brunch or Coriander Chicken Tikka for a summer holiday lunch. Bring back the Sunday roast with Roast Lamb with Fruity Herb Stuffing and swap the Friday night take-away for home-made Fish and Chips. There are plenty of dishes here for during the week too, including wonderful desserts such as Baked Bananas and Strawberry Tarts. So get cooking and try these great recipes. Your family will love them, and they'll love you for cooking them.

About Weight Watchers

For more than 40 years Weight Watchers has been helping people around the world to lose weight using a long term sustainable approach. Weight Watchers successful weight loss system is based on four tried and trusted principles:

- Eating healthily
- Being more active
- Adjusting behaviour to help weight loss
- Getting support in weekly meetings

Our unique **ProPoints** system empowers you to manage your food plan and make wise recipe choices for a healthier, happier you.

To find out more about Weight Watchers and the **ProPoints** values
for these recipes contact Customer Service on 0845 345 1500.

Storing and freezing

Many recipes in this book store well in the fridge, but make sure you use them up within a day or two. Some can also be frozen. Try doubling up the quantities in the recipes and storing the extra portions for another day. This way you'll always have a fantastic selection of meals that you can pull out and reheat, and you can be sure that your family is eating well, no matter how busy your day has been. However, if you do store and freeze food, it is important to make sure you know how to freeze safely.

- Wrap any food to be frozen in rigid containers or strong freezer bags. This is important to stop foods contaminating each other or getting freezer burn.
- Label the containers or bags with the contents and date – your freezer should have a star marking that tells you how long you can keep different types of frozen food.
- Never freeze warm food – always let it cool completely first.
- Never freeze food that has already been frozen and defrosted.
- Freeze food in portions, then you can take out as little or as much as you need each time.
- Defrost what you need in the fridge, making sure you put anything that might have juices, such as meat, on a covered plate or in a container.

- Fresh food, such as raw meat and fish, should be wrapped and frozen as soon as possible.
- Most fruit and vegetables can be frozen by open freezing. Lay them out on a tray, freeze until solid and then pack them into bags.
- Some vegetables, such as peas, broccoli and broad beans can be blanched first by cooking for 2 minutes in boiling water. Drain, refresh under cold water and then freeze once cold.

- Fresh herbs are great frozen – either seal leaves in bags or, for soft herbs such as basil and parsley, chop finely and add to ice cube trays with water. These are great for dropping into casseroles or soups straight from the freezer.

Some things cannot be frozen. Whole eggs do not freeze well, but yolks and whites can be frozen separately. Vegetables with a high water content, such as salad leaves, celery and cucumber, will not freeze. Fried foods will be soggy if frozen, and sauces such as mayonnaise will separate when thawed and should not be frozen.

Shopping hints and tips

Always buy the best ingredients you can afford. If you are going to cook healthy meals, it is worth investing in some quality ingredients that will really add flavour to your dishes. When buying meat, choose lean cuts of meat or lean mince, and if you are buying prepacked cooked sliced meat, buy it fresh from the deli counter.

When you're going around the supermarket it's tempting to pick up foods you like and put them in your trolley without thinking about how you will use them. So, a good plan is to decide what dishes you want to cook before you go shopping, check your store cupboard and make a list of what you need. You'll save time by not drifting aimlessly around the supermarket picking up what you fancy.

We've added a checklist here for some of the store cupboard ingredients used in this book. Just add fresh ingredients in your regular shop and you'll be ready to cook the wonderful recipes in *Family Favourites*.

Store cupboard checklist

- [ ] apricots, dried
- [ ] artificial sweetener
- [ ] baking powder
- [ ] bay leaves
- [ ] bicarbonate of soda
- [ ] brown sauce
- [ ] cannellini beans, canned
- [ ] capers, in a jar
- [ ] caraway seeds
- [ ] chick peas, canned
- [ ] chilli (flakes and powder)
- [ ] chocolate, plain
- [ ] cinnamon, ground
- [ ] cocoa powder
- [ ] coconut milk, reduced fat
- [ ] cooking spray, calorie controlled
- [ ] coriander, ground
- [ ] cornflour
- [ ] crab meat, canned
- [ ] cumin, ground
- [ ] curry pastes
- [ ] custard, low fat

- [ ] fish sauce
- [ ] flour (plain and self raising)
- [ ] garam masala
- [ ] herbs, dried
- [ ] honey, clear
- [ ] jam, reduced sugar
- [ ] jelly, sugar free
- [ ] kidney beans, canned
- [ ] lentils, dried
- [ ] mango chutney
- [ ] mayonnaise, reduced fat
- [ ] mustard (Dijon and wholegrain)
- [ ] noodles, dried
- [ ] nutmeg
- [ ] oil (olive and sesame)
- [ ] olives, black, in a jar
- [ ] paprika
- [ ] passata
- [ ] pasta, dried
- [ ] pearl barley, dried
- [ ] peppercorns
- [ ] peppers, in a jar

- [ ] pineapple chunks, canned in natural juice
- [ ] pizza base mix
- [ ] porridge oats
- [ ] rice, dried (basmati and risotto)
- [ ] saffron
- [ ] salt
- [ ] soy sauce
- [ ] spice blends
- [ ] stock cubes
- [ ] sugar
- [ ] Tabasco sauce
- [ ] teriyaki sauce
- [ ] tomato ketchup
- [ ] tomato purée
- [ ] tomatoes, canned
- [ ] trifle sponges
- [ ] tuna, canned in brine
- [ ] turmeric
- [ ] vanilla essence
- [ ] vinegar (balsamic and white wine)
- [ ] Worcestershire sauce

Brunches and lunches

Eggy crumpets 'n' bacon

Serves 4
222 calories per serving
Takes 20 minutes

2 eggs
2 tablespoons skimmed milk
1 teaspoon dried mixed herbs
4 x 46 g crumpets
200 g (7 oz) cherry tomatoes, halved
2 tablespoons brown sauce
2 teaspoons tomato purée
4 rashers smoked lean back bacon
calorie controlled cooking spray
freshly ground black pepper

This is ideal for a weekend breakfast.

1 Put the eggs and milk into a jug with the herbs and season with black pepper. Whisk until beaten. Put the crumpets into a shallow dish and pour over the eggs. Turn to coat in the mixture and then set aside.

2 Meanwhile, put the cherry tomatoes, brown sauce, tomato purée and 4 tablespoons of cold water into a small saucepan. Gently bubble for 3–5 minutes until the tomatoes are just soft. Set aside.

3 Preheat the grill to hot. Put the bacon on a grill pan and cook for 3–5 minutes until crispy. Meanwhile, heat a non stick frying pan and spray with the cooking spray. Gently cook the crumpets for 5 minutes, turning halfway, until golden and the eggs have set. Divide the crumpets between four plates and top with the crispy bacon and tomato sauce.

❤ **Variation...** For a vegetarian option, top the eggy crumpets with 50 g (1¾ oz) sliced mushrooms each, sautéed in calorie controlled cooking spray in step 3, instead of the bacon.

The ultimate hash browns

Serves 4
215 calories per serving
Takes 45 minutes

400 g (14 oz) potatoes, peeled and cut into large chunks
275 g (9½ oz) green vegetables, such as leeks and broccoli, chopped roughly
calorie controlled cooking spray
3 rashers lean back bacon, chopped roughly
1 teaspoon Dijon mustard
1 teaspoon wholegrain mustard
1 tablespoon white wine vinegar (optional)
4 eggs
salt and freshly ground black pepper

This is the perfect way to use up leftover vegetables. Serve with grilled tomatoes.

1 Bring a pan of water to the boil, add the potatoes and cook for 20 minutes or until tender. Drain and mash. At the same time, bring a second pan of water to the boil, add the green vegetables and cook for 4–5 minutes until tender. Drain thoroughly.

2 Meanwhile, heat a non stick frying pan and spray with the cooking spray. Gently cook the bacon for 5 minutes until crispy. Remove and drain on kitchen towel.

3 Put the green vegetables into a large bowl. Add the mashed potato, mustards and cooked bacon. Season and mix together.

4 Using wet hands, divide the mixture into four and then shape each quarter into a large patty or burger shape.

5 Heat the frying pan you cooked the bacon in and spray again with the cooking spray. Gently fry the potato cakes for 10 minutes, turning once (do not attempt to turn until after 5 minutes). Once cooked, transfer to a plate and keep warm.

6 Meanwhile, bring a shallow lidded pan of water to the boil, add the vinegar, if using, and reduce the heat to a steady simmer. Break the eggs into the water one at a time. Cover the pan and cook for 4 minutes. Remove the eggs with a slotted spoon and place on top of the hash browns. Season with black pepper and serve.

 Variation... For a vegetarian version, replace the bacon rashers with three Quorn Deli Bacon Style Rashers and cook according to the packet instructions.

Smoked haddock kedgeree

Serves 4

393 calories per serving

Takes 20 minutes to prepare, 30–35 minutes to cook

300 g (10½ oz) smoked haddock fillets

2 bay leaves

4 whole peppercorns

300 ml (10 fl oz) skimmed milk

a pinch of saffron strands

2 tablespoons boiling water

calorie controlled cooking spray

2 onions, chopped

225 g (8 oz) dried basmati rice

1 tablespoon garam masala

700 ml (1¼ pints) chicken or vegetable stock

a large bunch of fresh parsley, chopped finely, stalks included

200 g (7 oz) virtually fat free plain fromage frais

salt and freshly ground black pepper

To garnish

2 eggs

1 lemon, cut into wedges

A classic recipe using smoked haddock, this kedgeree is tasty and substantial. If you keep some smoked haddock fillets in the freezer, try the kedgeree for an impromptu Sunday brunch or quick supper standby.

1 Place the haddock fillets skin side up in a large pan with the bay leaves and peppercorns. Pour over the milk, bring to the boil and then turn off and leave to cool. Place the saffron strands in the boiling water to soak.

2 Meanwhile, heat a large non stick frying pan and spray with the cooking spray. Fry the onions until golden and softened, adding a splash of water if necessary to prevent them from sticking.

3 Add the rice, saffron strands with their soaking water and the garam masala, stirring to mix. Add the stock and bring to the boil, stirring occasionally. Turn down to a gentle simmer and leave to cook for 15 minutes.

4 Meanwhile, bring another small pan of water to the boil, add the eggs and simmer for 8 minutes to hard boil. When the eggs are cooked, plunge into cold water to cool, remove the shells and quarter.

5 Remove the haddock from the milk and flake with your fingers on to a plate, removing the skin and any bones as you go. Strain the milk, add it to the rice and stir in.

6 After about 15–20 minutes, when the rice is just cooked and most of the liquid absorbed, add the flaked haddock, parsley and fromage frais. Stir to heat through. Check the seasoning and serve garnished with the eggs and lemon wedges.

Banana pancakes with maple syrup

Serves 4

149 calories per serving

Takes 15 minutes to prepare,
10 minutes to cook

Ⓥ

50 g (1¾ oz) plain white flour
½ teaspoon baking powder
½ teaspoon bicarbonate of soda
½ teaspoon caster sugar
1 banana
1 egg, separated
1 teaspoon low fat spread
150 ml (5 fl oz) buttermilk
calorie controlled cooking spray
2 tablespoons maple syrup

Sometimes you need to push the boat out. So choose this for a brunch on a special day.

1 Sift the flour, baking powder and bicarbonate of soda into a bowl and add the sugar. Cut the banana in half. Roughly dice one half and thinly slice the other. Set aside.

2 In a clean, grease-free bowl, whisk the egg white until stiff peaks form.

3 Put the low fat spread into a large jug and microwave for a few seconds on high until melted. Add the buttermilk, egg yolk and the sliced banana. Using an electric whisk, whisk to create a thick, fairly smooth mixture. Pour this into the dry ingredients and gently mix together to form a batter. Using a metal spoon, fold the egg white into the mixture.

4 Heat a non stick frying pan to a medium heat and spray with the cooking spray. When hot, use half of the batter to make four pancakes. (They will be about 10 cm/4 inches across.) Cook for 2–3 minutes on each side, turning them gently with a large palette knife. When cooked, remove and keep warm while you cook the remaining batter.

5 Serve immediately by placing two pancakes each on four warm plates. Scatter the diced banana over them and drizzle ½ a tablespoon of maple syrup over the top of each serving.

Apricot turnovers

Serves 4

228 calories per serving

Takes 20 minutes to prepare
+ cooling, 15–20 minutes
to cook

Ⓥ

❄

240 g packet croissant dough

4 ready-to-eat dried apricots

**4 teaspoons Weight Watchers
Reduced Sugar Apricot Jam**

2 teaspoons icing sugar

*Serve with a small glass (100 ml/3½ fl oz) of orange juice
per person.*

1 Preheat the oven to Gas Mark 4/180°C/fan oven160°C.

2 Unroll the croissant dough and fold it in half. Roll out the
dough on a piece of non stick baking parchment until it
measures 60 x 15 cm (24 x 6 inches) and cut into four squares.
Take one square and fold in half diagonally to form a triangle.
Starting 1 cm (½ inch) in at the folded side, cut a 1 cm (½ inch)
wide border along the open sides. Leave 1 cm (½ inch) uncut
at the end so the strips remain attached.

3 Unfold the triangle. Lift the border strips up and slip one strip
under the other. Pull across the base to the opposite corner
and press the attached points of the strips to the corners of
the base to seal. Put one dried apricot into the centre and
transfer to a non stick baking tray. Repeat to make three more
turnovers. Bake in the oven for 15–20 minutes until golden and
cooked.

4 Meanwhile, melt the apricot jam in a small pan.

5 Once the turnovers are cooked, drizzle 1 teaspoon of the jam
over each dried apricot. Leave to cool and then dust with the
icing sugar.

Oven-baked tomatoes and eggs

Serves 4
227 calories per serving
Takes 15 minutes to prepare,
 35 minutes to cook
Ⓨ

**calorie controlled cooking
 spray**
**600 g (1 lb 5 oz) potatoes,
 peeled and diced**
8 tomatoes, halved
4 fresh thyme sprigs
4 eggs
freshly ground black pepper
**2 tablespoons snipped fresh
 chives, to serve**

An easy and satisfying brunch for the whole family.

1 Preheat the oven to Gas Mark 6/200°C/fan oven 180°C.
Spray a small non stick roasting tin with the cooking spray.
Add the potatoes, stir and spray again to thoroughly coat. Bake
for 20 minutes and then stir before adding the tomatoes and
thyme sprigs. Roast for a further 15 minutes until the potatoes
are tender and the tomatoes are beginning to char. Season with
black pepper.

2 Meanwhile, bring a shallow lidded pan of water to the boil,
reduce the heat to a steady simmer and break the eggs into
the water one at a time. Cover the pan and cook for 4 minutes.
Remove the eggs with a slotted spoon.

3 Serve the potatoes and tomatoes on warmed plates with a
poached egg on top. Sprinkle with the chives.

Variation... If you prefer, use 20 small vine tomatoes to
share between four, instead of eight tomatoes, roasting
them on the vine.

Minestrone soup

Serves 4
265 calories per serving
Takes 20 minutes to prepare,
   15 minutes to cook
❄

1 teaspoon olive oil
4 rashers smoked lean back
   bacon, cut into strips
2 onions, chopped finely
1 celery stick, diced
2 garlic cloves, chopped
100 g (3½ oz) potatoes, peeled
   and diced
250 g (9 oz) swede, peeled and
   diced
2 carrots, peeled and diced
2 tomatoes, chopped
100 g (3½ oz) dried small
   pasta shapes
1.3 litres (2½ pints) vegetable
   or chicken stock
salt and freshly ground black
   pepper
a handful of chopped fresh
   parsley, to garnish

*This soup is a meal in itself, with lots of chunky vegetables
and pasta. It makes a satisfying lunchtime meal.*

1 Heat the oil in a large, lidded, non stick saucepan and add
the bacon and onions. Cook for 4–5 minutes, until the onions
are softened.

2 Add the celery, garlic, potatoes, swede, carrots, tomatoes
and pasta. Stir thoroughly. Pour in the stock, cover and cook for
15 minutes until the vegetables are soft.

3 Season and serve in four warmed bowls, garnished with the
parsley.

🅥 **Variation...** For a vegetarian option, omit the bacon and
use vegetable stock.

Quick tomato soup

Serves 4

90 calories per serving

Takes 10 minutes to prepare,
  15 minutes to cook

Ⓥ

❄

1 large onion, chopped

2 celery sticks, chopped

2 garlic cloves, crushed

450 ml (16 fl oz) hot vegetable
  stock

2 x 400 g cans chopped
  tomatoes

2 tablespoons tomato purée

1 tablespoon dried mixed
  herbs

1 teaspoon dark or light
  muscovado sugar

1 tablespoon cornflour

salt and freshly ground black
  pepper

To serve

4 tablespoons low fat natural
  yogurt

celery leaves (optional)

*Everyone loves tomato soup and this home-made version
tastes fantastic.*

1 Put the onion, celery and garlic in a large saucepan and
pour in the hot stock. Bring to the boil, reduce the heat and
simmer for 5 minutes.

2 Add the chopped tomatoes, tomato purée, herbs and sugar.
Bring to the boil once more and then reduce the heat. Simmer
for 5 minutes.

3 Transfer the soup to a blender or use a hand blender and
whizz for about 15 seconds, until smooth.

4 Pour the soup back into the saucepan, if necessary. Blend
the cornfour to a paste with 3 tablespoons of cold water
and stir into the soup. Reheat gently, stirring constantly until
the soup thickens slightly. Cook for another minute or two.
Season to taste and serve in warmed bowls topped with a
tablespoon of yogurt, a few celery leaves, if using, and a little
more black pepper.

Tip... Try using canned whole plum tomatoes in this recipe
– chop them roughly first. This only takes a few moments
and it makes the recipe more economical.

Variation... To make a cream of tomato soup, add 200 g
(7 oz) low fat soft cheese when blending.

Baked cheesy pots

Serves 4
125 calories per serving
Takes 20 minutes

**calorie controlled cooking
  spray**
3 eggs, separated
**100 g (3½ oz) onion and chive
  cottage cheese**
**2 spring onions, chopped
  finely**
**100 g (3½ oz) low fat soft
  cheese**
35 g (1¼ oz) diced lean ham
**salt and freshly ground black
  pepper**

*These scrummy little pots are delicious served with grilled
cherry tomatoes on the side.*

1 Preheat the oven to Gas Mark 5/190°C/fan oven 170°C.
Spray four 200 ml (7 fl oz) ovenproof ramekins with the cooking
spray and put them on a baking tray. Set aside.

2 In a clean, grease-free bowl, whisk the egg whites until
they form stiff peaks. In another bowl, mix together the
cottage cheese, spring onions, soft cheese, ham and egg
yolks. Season generously.

3 With a large metal spoon, fold the egg whites into the
cheese mixture until just combined. Divide between the
ramekins and bake in the oven for 10 minutes until golden
and risen. Serve immediately.

Tuna pasta Niçoise

Serves 4
424 calories per serving
Takes 20 minutes

225 g (8 oz) dried conchiglie
4 eggs
200 g (7 oz) fine green beans, halved
50 g (1¾ oz) watercress
1 Little Gem lettuce, shredded
4 large vine-ripened tomatoes, cut into wedges
1 small red onion, sliced thinly into rings
200 g can tuna in brine, drained and flaked
salt and freshly ground black pepper

For the dressing
4 tablespoons reduced fat mayonnaise
3 tablespoons skimmed milk
1 teaspoon clear honey
juice of ½ a lemon

Pasta, tuna and hard boiled eggs help to turn this substantial salad into a main meal.

1 Bring a pan of water to the boil, add the pasta and eggs and cook for 8 minutes. Remove the eggs from the water and set aside. Continue cooking the pasta according to the packet instructions or until al dente. Once the pasta is cooked, drain and cool under cold running water. Drain again.

2 Meanwhile, bring a second pan of water to the boil, add the beans and cook for 4–5 minutes or until tender. Drain and cool under cold running water. Drain again.

3 Place the watercress and lettuce on a serving plate and top with the cold pasta and beans, tomatoes, onion and tuna. Peel the eggs and cut in half. Arrange on top of the salad and season well.

4 In a bowl, mix together the ingredients for the dressing and season. Drizzle over the salad and serve.

Coriander chicken tikka

Serves 4
193 calories per serving
Takes 20 minutes
❄

**4 x 150 g (5½ oz) skinless
boneless chicken breasts,
each cut into 3 or 4 slices**

For the marinade

**1 red chilli, de-seeded and
chopped**

2 spring onions, sliced

**½ x 25 g packet fresh
coriander**

**2 teaspoons tandoori spice
blend**

2 tablespoons mango chutney

1 teaspoon garam masala

**2 tablespoons low fat natural
yogurt**

juice of a lemon

*Serve with a generous salad, or use to fill two medium
slices of bread with ½ tablespoon reduced fat mayonnaise
per person and lettuce.*

1 Preheat the grill to hot. Put the chilli, spring onions and
coriander in a food processor and whizz until finely chopped.
Add the tandoori spice blend, mango chutney and garam
masala and whizz again. Add the yogurt and lemon juice and
whizz again until combined.

2 Transfer the marinade to a bowl and add the chicken pieces.
Turn to coat in the yogurt mixture.

3 Arrange the chicken pieces on a foil-lined grill tray and cook
under the grill for 10 minutes, turning until cooked and charred.
Serve immediately.

Satay chicken

Serves 4

345 calories per serving

Takes 35 minutes + marinating

4 x 175 g (6 oz) skinless boneless chicken breasts, sliced into long strips

lime wedges, to serve (optional)

For the marinade

2 garlic cloves, crushed

2.5 cm (1 inch) fresh root ginger, grated

2 tablespoons soy sauce

1 tablespoon clear honey

For the satay sauce

6 teaspoons crunchy peanut butter

1 small red chilli, de-seeded and chopped finely

juice of 2 limes

4 tablespoons vegetable or chicken stock

2 tablespoons reduced fat coconut milk

salt and freshly ground black pepper

Satays are always popular served as finger food at parties, but they also make a tasty lunch with a crisp salad.

1 Mix together the marinade ingredients in a bowl and add the chicken strips. Mix together well to ensure that the chicken is coated and leave to marinate in the fridge for at least 30 minutes but preferably overnight.

2 Make the sauce by blending all the ingredients together either in a food processor or just in a bowl. Cover with cling film and keep in the refrigerator until ready to use.

3 Soak 20 wooden skewers in cold water for 10 minutes. Preheat the grill to high. Thread the chicken on to the skewers and grill for 3 minutes on each side until golden brown and cooked through. Keep brushing with the leftover marinade.

4 Serve the chicken satay skewers with the peanut sauce as a dip and lime wedges to squeeze over, if using.

Variation... You could use 700 g (1 lb 9 oz) extra lean pork, turkey, lamb or braising steak instead of the chicken.

Spicy crab cakes

Serves 4

265 calories per serving

Takes 40 minutes +
  30 minutes chilling
  (optional)

- **250 g (9 oz) potatoes, peeled and diced**
- **2 red peppers, de-seeded and halved**
- **4 medium slices white bread**
- **1 egg, beaten**
- **2 x 120 g cans white crab meat, drained**
- **2 spring onions, chopped finely**
- **½ teaspoon chilli powder or 1 small red chilli, de-seeded and chopped finely**
- **a bunch of fresh coriander, chopped**
- **1 tablespoon Worcestershire sauce**
- **grated zest and juice of 2 limes**
- **4 drops Tabasco sauce**
- **1 teaspoon English mustard**
- **calorie controlled cooking spray**
- **salt and freshly ground black pepper**

Crab cakes make a special brunch dish, and if you're using canned crab they needn't be expensive at all. Serve with a soy dipping sauce or sweet chilli sauce and a crisp salad.

1 Bring a pan of water to the boil, add the potatoes and cook for 20 minutes or until tender. Drain.

2 Meanwhile, place the peppers cut side down on the grill pan and grill them under a high heat until the skins are blackened and blistered. Place them in a plastic bag and leave to cool. Using a food processor, whizz the bread to breadcrumbs.

3 Mix the potatoes and breadcrumbs together with all the remaining ingredients, except the cooking spray. When the peppers are cool enough to handle, peel away the skins and chop the flesh finely. Add to the potato and crab cake mixture and mix it all together.

4 Using wet hands, make the mixture into eight patties and, if you have time, place on a tray in the fridge to firm up for 30 minutes. Otherwise cook them immediately in a non stick frying pan sprayed with the cooking spray, frying for 4–5 minutes on either side until golden brown and cooked through. You may need to do this in two batches.

Tip... Handle the crab cakes carefully if they have not been chilled as they will break up easily.

Kebabs with mint and yogurt dip

Serves 4

265 calories per serving

Takes 30 minutes + marinating

❄

400 g (14 oz) lean beef steak, trimmed of visible fat and cubed

200 g (7 oz) button mushrooms

8 bay leaves

For the marinade

2 tablespoons olive oil

1 tablespoon red wine

1 large red chilli, de-seeded and chopped finely

1 tablespoon ground cumin

2 garlic cloves, crushed

salt and freshly ground black pepper

For the dip

300 g (10½ oz) low fat natural yogurt

a bunch of fresh mint, chopped finely

½ cucumber, peeled, de-seeded and chopped finely

Cooked either on a barbecue or under the grill this hot, cumin and garlic flavoured beef stays moist and tender. Serve with a medium pitta bread per person and a green salad.

1 Mix all the marinade ingredients together in a shallow bowl and mix in the beef, mushrooms and bay leaves. Cover and marinate in the refrigerator for at least 1 hour, preferably overnight.

2 Make the dip by mixing together all the ingredients and pouring into a serving bowl. Refrigerate before serving.

3 To cook the kebabs, prepare the barbecue or heat the grill to high, thread the meat, mushrooms and bay leaves alternately on to skewers and grill for 5–10 minutes, turning once, until cooked through.

4 Serve the kebabs, pushed off the skewers, with the dip.

Tip... If using wooden skewers, soak them in water for 10 minutes beforehand to prevent them from burning.

Cheese, onion and tomato quiche

Serves 4

350 calories per serving

Takes 20 minutes to prepare, 20–25 minutes to cook

Ⓥ

❄

For the pastry

8 x 15 g (½ oz) sheets filo pastry, measuring 30 x 40 cm (12 x 16 inches)

2 tablespoons light olive oil

For the filling

2 teaspoons olive oil

2 large onions, sliced into rings

3 large tomatoes, sliced

2 eggs

150 ml (5 fl oz) skimmed milk

1 tablespoon chopped fresh mixed herbs or 1 teaspoon dried mixed herbs

40 g (1½ oz) half fat mature Cheddar cheese, grated

salt and freshly ground black pepper

Filo pastry gives a new slant to an old favourite. Serve with a large mixed salad with fat free dressing.

1 Preheat the oven to Gas Mark 2/150°C/fan oven 130°C.

2 Unroll the sheets of filo pastry, keeping them covered with cling film or a damp cloth as you work to prevent them drying out. Brush each one with a little olive oil and layer them in a 20 cm (8 inch) flan tin. Stand the flan tin on a baking tray.

3 For the filling, heat the oil in a non stick frying pan and sauté the onions until softened, about 5 minutes. Tip them into the flan case and spread them over the base. Top with the sliced tomatoes.

4 Beat together the eggs, milk and herbs. Season and pour into the flan case. Sprinkle with the cheese and bake for 20–25 minutes on the middle shelf until set. Cool slightly before serving.

Variation... If you're not keen on tomatoes, use a couple of sliced courgettes or 175 g (6 oz) lightly cooked asparagus instead.

Marvellous meat

Spaghetti bolognese

Serves 4

420 calories per serving

Takes 20 minutes to prepare,
1 hour to cook

❄

1 teaspoon olive oil

1 red onion, chopped finely

1 garlic clove, crushed

225 g (8 oz) lean minced beef

2 rashers smoked streaky
bacon, diced

2 celery sticks, sliced

1 carrot, peeled and chopped
finely

150 g (5½ oz) button
mushrooms, diced

1 teaspoon dried mixed herbs

1 beef stock cube, crumbled

2 tablespoons tomato purée

100 ml (3½ fl oz) red wine

300 ml (10 fl oz) boiling water

400 g can chopped tomatoes

225 g (8 oz) dried spaghetti

2 tablespoons chopped fresh
parsley (optional)

salt and freshly ground black
pepper

Everyone loves a great spaghetti bolognese.

1 Heat the olive oil in a large non stick pan and cook the onion and garlic until softened. Add the minced beef and bacon and cook for a further 5 minutes until evenly browned.

2 Stir in the celery, carrot, mushrooms and herbs and cook for 2 minutes.

3 Mix together the crumbled stock cube, tomato purée, red wine and boiling water and pour into the pan with the chopped tomatoes. Stir well, season to taste and bring to the boil. Simmer for 50 minutes.

4 About 10 minutes before the bolognese is ready, bring a large pan of water to the boil. Add the pasta and cook until tender or according to the packet instructions. Drain and toss with the chopped parsley, if using.

5 Divide the pasta between four warmed serving plates and top with the bolognese sauce to serve.

Mini toad in the hole

Serves 4

114 calories per serving

Takes 15 minutes to prepare,
  18–20 minutes to cook

1 tablespoon sunflower oil
12 thin reduced fat pork
  sausages
1 large onion, sliced
125 g (4½ oz) plain white flour
1 egg
300 ml (10 fl oz) skimmed milk
salt and freshly ground black
  pepper

A fun way to serve up this family favourite; just add gravy and your favourite vegetables.

1 Preheat the oven to Gas Mark 7/220°C/fan oven 200°C.

2 Divide the oil between the hollows in a 12 hole muffin tin (¼ teaspoon in each) and heat in the oven for 2 minutes.

3 Twist each of the sausages in half to form two cocktail size sausages and snip to separate.

4 Place two sausages and some onion in each hollow and cook in the oven for 8 minutes until lightly browned.

5 Sift the flour into a bowl and season. Make a well in the centre, break in the egg and gradually whisk in the milk to give a smooth batter. Transfer to a jug.

6 When the sausages and onions are browned, pour in the batter, dividing it equally between the hollows. Return to the oven and cook for 18–20 minutes until the batters are risen, crisp and a rich golden brown. Serve three puddings per person.

❂ **Variation...** For a vegetarian version, use eight veggie sausages, each cut into three chunks. Place two chunks in each hollow of the muffin tin and follow the rest of the method above.

Shepherd's pie

Serves 4

390 calories per serving

Takes 20 minutes to prepare,
   1 hour to cook

❄

**900 g (2 lb) potatoes, peeled
   and quartered**

**350 g (12 oz) lean minced
   lamb**

1 large onion, chopped finely

1 large leek, chopped finely

1 carrot, peeled and chopped

**225 g (8 oz) swede or turnip,
   peeled and chopped**

**450 ml (16 fl oz) lamb or
   vegetable stock**

2 tablespoons cornflour

6 tablespoons skimmed milk

**salt and freshly ground black
   pepper**

*Serve with plenty of steamed vegetables: broccoli,
cauliflower or cabbage would be ideal.*

1 Bring a pan of water to the boil, add the potatoes and cook
for about 20 minutes, until tender.

2 Meanwhile, heat a large, lidded, non stick pan and add the
lamb, a handful at a time, cooking over a high heat to seal and
brown it and breaking it up with a spoon.

3 Add the onion, leek, carrot and swede or turnip and cook for
about 3 minutes, stirring often. Pour in the stock, bring to the
boil, cover and simmer for about 20 minutes.

4 Preheat the oven to Gas Mark 5/190°C/fan oven 170°C. Mix
the cornflour to a paste with 3–4 tablespoons of cold water.

5 Stir the blended cornflour into the lamb mixture. Cook until
thickened for about 2 minutes and then remove from the heat.

6 Drain the potatoes and mash them. Add the milk and
seasoning and beat vigorously with a wooden spoon until the
potatoes are light and fluffy. Alternatively, use a hand whisk to
whisk the potatoes for a few moments.

7 Transfer the lamb mixture to a 1.2 litre (2 pint) ovenproof
dish and top with the mashed potato. Bake for 25–30 minutes
until thoroughly heated and browned.

Variations... Before baking in the oven, sprinkle the surface
of the mash with a finely sliced leek and 25 g (1 oz) grated,
half fat, mature Cheddar cheese.

Ⓥ For a vegetarian version, use Quorn mince instead of
lamb and be sure to use vegetable stock.

Sweet and sour pork noodles

Serves 4
395 calories per serving
Takes 40 minutes
❄

225 g (8 oz) dried medium egg
   noodles

1 teaspoon sesame oil

calorie controlled cooking
   spray

350 g (12 oz) pork tenderloin,
   trimmed of visible fat and
   cut into thin strips

2 garlic cloves, crushed

225 g (8 oz) canned pineapple
   chunks in natural juice,
   drained and juice reserved

3 tablespoons soy sauce

2 tablespoons tomato purée

1 tablespoon cornflour

1 teaspoon white wine vinegar

1 green pepper, de-seeded and
   sliced

150 g (5½ oz) carrots, peeled
   and cut into matchsticks

150 g (5½ oz) courgettes,
   sliced

*This dish freezes well; divide it into individual portions
and pop in the freezer for when you want a quick and
easy meal.*

1 Bring a pan of water to the boil, add the noodles and cook
for 2 minutes or according to the packet instructions. Drain
well and mix in the sesame oil. Set aside.

2 Spray a wok or large non stick frying pan with the cooking
spray and stir-fry the pork and garlic for 5 minutes. Add the
pineapple chunks to the pan.

3 Mix the reserved pineapple juice with the soy sauce,
tomato purée, cornflour and vinegar to make a sweet and
sour mixture and set aside.

4 Add the pepper, carrots and courgettes to the pan and
stir-fry for a further 5 minutes. Stir in the sweet and sour
sauce and cook, stirring, until the sauce thickens.

5 Add the cooked noodles to the pan and heat through for
2–3 minutes. Serve on four warmed plates.

Tip... When you need to slice meat really thinly, freeze it for
about half an hour beforehand and it will be much easier
to handle.

Variation... Add a teaspoon of hot chilli sauce to the sweet
and sour mixture for an added zing.

Chilli con carne

Serves 4
305 calories per serving
Takes 25 minutes to prepare,
  1 hour to cook
❄

**350 g (12 oz) extra lean
  minced beef**
**1 tablespoon mild chilli
  powder**
1 teaspoon ground coriander
1 onion, chopped
2 garlic cloves, crushed
**175 g (6 oz) carrots, peeled
  and diced finely**
**100 g (3½ oz) button
  mushrooms, quartered**
100 ml (3½ fl oz) red wine
400 g can chopped tomatoes
2 tablespoons tomato purée
300 ml (10 fl oz) beef stock
**410 g can kidney beans,
  drained and rinsed**
**salt and freshly ground black
  pepper**
**2 tablespoons chopped fresh
  parsley, to garnish**

*The great thing about this dish is that it needs very little
attention, so you can spend time with the family while it
cooks.*

1 Heat a large non stick saucepan and add the mince. Dry-fry
for 2–3 minutes until it is browned. Add the chilli powder,
coriander, onion, garlic, carrots and mushrooms and stir well.
Cook, stirring, for 5 minutes.

2 Pour in the wine, chopped tomatoes, tomato purée and stock,
season, stir well and bring to the boil. Reduce the heat and
simmer, stirring from time to time, for 1 hour.

3 About 5 minutes before the end of the cooking time, stir in
the kidney beans. Allow them to heat through.

4 Ladle the chilli into warmed bowls, sprinkle with the
chopped parsley and serve.

Tip... Make this as hot as you want, but take care. Add a
little chilli powder first and then taste before adding more;
it's worth remembering that the heat of the chilli develops
as it cooks.

Ⓥ **Variation...** To make a vegetarian version of this chilli,
use vegetarian mince and vegetable stock. You'll only need
to cook the chilli for 30 minutes.

Roast lamb with fruity herb stuffing

Serves 4

312 calories per serving

Takes 20 minutes to prepare
+ 10–15 minutes resting,
1½–1¾ hours to cook

calorie controlled cooking
  spray

1 small onion, chopped finely

1 egg white, beaten lightly

60 g (2 oz) fresh white
  breadcrumbs

40 g (1½ oz) ready-to-eat
  semi-dried apricots, diced

2 heaped tablespoons
  chopped fresh parsley

1 tablespoon chopped fresh
  lemon thyme

finely grated zest and juice of
  ½ a lemon

650 g (1 lb 7 oz) boneless
  lamb leg joint, trimmed of
  visible fat

salt and freshly ground black
  pepper

Serve this fabulous joint for a family Sunday lunch with steamed vegetables of your choice.

1 Preheat the oven to Gas Mark 5/190°C/fan oven 170°C. Heat a lidded non stick saucepan until hot and spray with the cooking spray. Add the onion with 4 tablespoons of water. Cover and cook for 5 minutes over a medium heat until softened.

2 Meanwhile, make the stuffing. Mix the egg white with the breadcrumbs, apricots, herbs, lemon zest and lemon juice and season. Add the cooked onion.

3 Unroll the lamb on a chopping board so that it lies flat. Carefully slice through the lamb from the centre towards the sides, opening out the lamb horizontally like the jacket cover of a book.

4 Press the stuffing on to the lamb joint and then re-roll and secure with string in three or four places. Place in a non stick roasting tin, season and cover loosely with foil. Roast for 1¼ hours for slightly pink lamb, or 1½ hours for well done. Remove the foil and roast for a final 15 minutes to brown the joint. Rest for 10–15 minutes before carving into slices. Serve three medium slices of stuffed lamb per person.

Chorizo pizza with warm potato salad

Serves 4

300 calories per serving

Takes 25 minutes to prepare,
15–20 minutes to cook

**calorie controlled cooking
spray**

144 g packet pizza base mix

For the topping

2 onions, sliced

**1 teaspoon fresh rosemary
leaves, chopped**

**110 g (4 oz) chorizo sausage,
chopped into 2 cm (¾ inch)
dice**

10 cherry tomatoes, halved

For the salad

**450 g (1 lb) new potatoes,
scrubbed and chopped if
large**

**3 tablespoons fat free
dressing**

**2 tablespoons capers, drained
and chopped**

**1 tablespoon shredded fresh
mint leaves**

**salt and freshly ground black
pepper**

*Home-made pizzas are really easy to put together and so
much more fun than shop-bought ones.*

1 Preheat the oven to Gas Mark 7/220°C/fan oven 200°C.
Spray a non stick baking tray with the cooking spray and set
aside.

2 Prepare the pizza base according to the packet instructions.
Make a 24 cm (9½ inch) round and place it on the baking tray.

3 Spray a non stick frying pan with the cooking spray and
heat. Add the onions and stir-fry over a medium heat for
5 minutes until softened and beginning to brown. Add a splash
of water if necessary to prevent them from sticking. Add the
rosemary and let the onions cool slightly.

4 Spread the onions over the pizza base and top with the
chorizo and tomatoes. Bake for 15–20 minutes until golden.

5 Meanwhile, prepare the salad. Bring a lidded pan of water
to the boil, add the potatoes, cover and reduce the heat to
simmering. Cook for 10–15 minutes until tender. Drain. Mix in
the dressing, capers and mint and season. Divide the pizza into
four and serve with the salad.

Spicy meatballs

Serves 4

262 calories per serving

Takes 20 minutes to prepare,
  30 minutes to cook

❄

calorie controlled cooking
  spray

1 large onion, chopped finely

1 garlic clove, crushed

1 tablespoon medium curry
  powder

2 teaspoons ground cumin

400 g can chopped tomatoes

300 ml (10 fl oz) hot beef
  stock

75 g (2¾ oz) fresh wholemeal
  breadcrumbs

2 tablespoons skimmed milk

500 g (1 lb 2 oz) lean minced
  beef

1 tablespoon chopped fresh
  coriander (optional), plus
  extra to serve

freshly ground black pepper

Serve with 60 g (2 oz) dried brown rice per person, cooked according to the packet instructions.

1 For the sauce, heat a lidded flameproof casserole on the hob and spray with the cooking spray. Add the onion, cook for 4 minutes and then add the garlic, curry powder and 1 teaspoon of cumin. Cook for 1 minute, stirring. Add the tomatoes and stock, bring to the boil and simmer briskly, uncovered, for 10 minutes.

2 Meanwhile, mix the breadcrumbs and milk in a bowl and add the remaining cumin, the minced beef and the coriander, if using. Season with black pepper. Using wet hands, shape the mixture into 24 meatballs. Heat a large non stick frying pan and spray with the cooking spray. Add the meatballs and brown for about 5 minutes, turning to colour evenly.

3 Add the meatballs to the sauce and simmer, partially covered, for 30 minutes. Serve topped with extra coriander, if using.

Creamy lamb korma

Serves 4
306 calories per serving
Takes 1 hour

50 g (1¾ oz) unsalted cashew nuts

400 g (14 oz) lean boneless lamb leg steak, trimmed of visible fat and cubed

1 teaspoon turmeric

calorie controlled cooking spray

2 tablespoons korma curry paste

200 ml (7 fl oz) lamb stock

410 g can chick peas, drained and rinsed

100 g (3½ oz) low fat soft cheese

2 tablespoons chopped fresh coriander, to garnish

Serve with lots of spinach cooked with garlic and dried chilli flakes and a Weight Watchers plain poppadom per person.

1 Heat a deep, lidded, non stick saucepan and dry-fry the cashew nuts for 1–2 minutes until golden. Remove to a board and chop roughly. In a bowl, mix the lamb cubes with the turmeric.

2 Heat the pan again and spray with the cooking spray. Cook the lamb for 5 minutes, until brown all over. You may need to do this in batches. Return all the lamb to the pan. Add the curry paste and half the cashew nuts and cook for 2 minutes.

3 Stir in the stock, bring to the boil and simmer for 40 minutes, until the lamb is really tender. Stir in the chick peas and soft cheese and gently heat until thickened. Serve immediately, sprinkled with the coriander and remaining cashew nuts.

Venison casserole

Serves 4

210 calories per serving

Takes 15 minutes to prepare,
2 hours to cook

❄

350 g (12 oz) venison shoulder, trimmed of visible fat and diced

4 carrots, peeled and cut into matchsticks

1 onion, diced

100 g (3½ oz) button mushrooms, wiped

1 garlic clove, crushed

1 orange

250 ml (9 fl oz) red wine

1 tablespoon redcurrant jelly

1 tablespoon sauce flour

Don't worry if the sauce flour seems lumpy when initially added to the casserole; keep stirring and it will dissolve.

1 Preheat the oven to Gas Mark 4/180°C/fan oven 160°C.

2 Put the venison and vegetables into a large, lidded, ovenproof casserole dish with the garlic.

3 Cut two slices from the orange and cut each slice in half. Add to the casserole dish.

4 Juice the rest of the orange, add to the red wine and make the liquid up to 400 ml (14 fl oz) with water. Pour into the casserole and cover. Cook for 1½ hours.

5 Add the redcurrant jelly and sauce flour and stir well. Cook for a further 30 minutes before serving.

Variation... Substitute 340 g (12 oz) diced lean braising steak for the venison and 200 g (8 oz) drained prunes in natural juice for the orange.

Sausage casserole

Serves 4

210 calories per serving

Takes 20 minutes to prepare,
45 minutes to cook

calorie controlled cooking spray
1 large onion, chopped
275 g (9½ oz) reduced fat pork sausages, halved
1 red pepper, de-seeded and sliced
1 Savoy cabbage, shredded
400 g can chopped tomatoes
1½ teaspoons caraway seeds
salt and freshly ground black pepper

A comforting and filling casserole that is perfect for all the family.

1 Preheat the oven to Gas Mark 4/180°C/fan oven 160°C.

2 Spray a lidded flameproof casserole dish with the cooking spray and cook the onion over a medium heat for 3–4 minutes. Add the sausages and cook, turning them occasionally, until they are brown all over.

3 Add the pepper, cabbage, tomatoes, caraway seeds, 4 tablespoons of water and some seasoning. Mix well. Bring it all to a gentle simmer and then cover the dish and transfer to the oven.

4 Cook for 30 minutes and then remove from the oven and stir. Return to the oven and cook for another 15 minutes. Serve hot.

Fresh pea and ham pasta

Serves 4
380 calories per serving
Takes 25 minutes

240 g (8½ oz) dried pasta
  shells
calorie controlled cooking
  spray
2 onions, chopped finely
300 g (10½ oz) frozen petit
  pois, defrosted
1 small lettuce, shredded
1 teaspoon caster sugar
200 g (7 oz) lean honey roast
  ham, cut into strips
4 tablespoons half fat crème
  fraîche
25 g packet fresh mint,
  chopped
salt and freshly ground black
  pepper

*This sauce will bring back the flavours of summer all
year round.*

1 Bring a pan of water to the boil, add the pasta and cook
according to the packet instructions. Drain.

2 Meanwhile, heat a large, lidded, non stick pan, spray with
the cooking spray and fry the onions until soft. Add the petit
pois, lettuce, sugar and 2 tablespoons of water. Season, cover
and cook for 10 minutes.

3 Stir in the ham, crème fraîche, mint and cooked pasta.
Check the seasoning and serve.

Steak fajitas

Serves 4

385 calories per serving

Takes 10 minutes to prepare +
1 hour marinating,
10 minutes to cook

**175 g (6 oz) lean braising
steak, trimmed of visible fat
and cut into strips**

juice of a lime

1–2 garlic cloves, crushed

2 teaspoons olive oil

8 small soft flour tortillas

**1 green pepper, de-seeded and
cut into strips**

**1 red pepper, de-seeded and
cut into strips**

**125 g (4½ oz) button
mushrooms, sliced**

1 onion, sliced

2 tomatoes, sliced

**salt and freshly ground black
pepper**

*This is a quick and easy recipe for those with a busy
lifestyle. Serve with a green leafy salad.*

1 Put the steak into a bowl with the lime juice, garlic and
1 teaspoon of olive oil. Cover and refrigerate for about 1 hour.

2 Preheat the oven to Gas Mark 4/180°C/fan oven 160°C.
Wrap the tortillas in foil and warm them in the oven for about
10 minutes.

3 Meanwhile, heat a wok or large non stick frying pan and
add the remaining oil. Stir-fry the marinated steak for 2 minutes
and then add all the vegetables and stir-fry for a further
4–5 minutes. Season.

4 Divide the stir-fry between the warmed tortillas, roll up and
serve two fajitas per person.

Variation... Use turkey or chicken stir-fry strips instead
of steak.

Family beef cobbler

Serves 4

376 calories per serving

Takes 15 minutes to prepare,
  1½ hours to cook

❄

**400 g (14 oz) lean braising
  beef, cut into chunks**

300 ml (10 fl oz) beef stock

2 onions, sliced

**2 large carrots, peeled and
  sliced**

2 celery sticks, sliced

200 g can chopped tomatoes

**2 tablespoons dried pearl
  barley**

2 bay leaves

**½ tablespoon dried mixed
  herbs**

75 g (2¾ oz) self raising flour

¼ teaspoon baking powder

20 g (¾ oz) low fat spread

**2 teaspoons wholegrain
  mustard**

**1 tablespoon chopped fresh
  parsley**

½ tablespoon skimmed milk

**1 large swede, peeled and
  diced**

**salt and freshly ground black
  pepper**

*A wonderful dish for winter, this casserole is topped with
savoury scones.*

1 Preheat the oven to Gas Mark 4/180°C/fan oven 160°C.

2 Put the beef, stock, vegetables, pearl barley, bay leaves and
herbs in a large, lidded, ovenproof casserole dish and season
well. Cover, place in the oven and cook for 1 hour, stirring
occasionally.

3 Just before the end of the hour, prepare the topping. Sieve
the flour and baking powder into a bowl and rub in the low fat
spread until the mixture resembles fine breadcrumbs. Add the
mustard and parsley and mix thoroughly.

4 Add just enough cold water to form a soft but not sticky
dough. Use your hands to roughly shape the dough into a fat
sausage about 10 cm (4 inches) long. Cut this into eight thin
round scones (or four thicker ones if you prefer).

5 Pop the scones on top of the casserole and brush them
with the milk. Return the casserole to the oven, uncovered,
and cook for a further 25–30 minutes until the scones are
risen and golden.

6 Meanwhile, bring a pan of water to the boil, add the swede
and cook until it is tender. Drain, mash and serve with the
casserole and scones in four warmed shallow bowls.

Perfect poultry

Roast chicken with rosemary and lemon potatoes

Serves 4

345 calories per serving

Takes 15 minutes to prepare,
1 hour 35 minutes to cook

400 g (14 oz) potatoes, peeled and cut into wedges

1.5 kg (3 lb 5 oz) whole chicken

2 lemons, 1 cut into wedges the other cut in half

a small bunch of fresh rosemary, leaves chopped

calorie controlled cooking spray

300 ml (10 fl oz) chicken stock

salt and freshly ground black pepper

1 Bring a pan of water to the boil, add the potatoes and cook for 15–20 minutes until just tender. Drain well.

2 Preheat the oven to Gas Mark 6/200°C/fan oven 180°C. Place the chicken in a large non stick roasting tin and season all over. Squeeze the juice from the halved lemon over the skin of the chicken and then place the squeezed lemon 'shells' inside the cavity with half the rosemary.

3 Place the lemon wedges and potatoes around the bird. Spray with the cooking spray, season and sprinkle with the remaining rosemary. Roast for 1¼ hours, basting occasionally with any juices in the tin, turning and basting the potatoes too. To test if the chicken is cooked, stick a skewer or knife into the meatiest portion of one of the thighs. The juices should run clear.

4 When cooked, remove the chicken from the roasting tin to a carving board, cover with foil and keep warm while you make the gravy.

5 To make the gravy, remove the potatoes and lemon wedges to serving bowls and keep warm. Drain off any excess fat and place the roasting tin on the hob. Heat until the juices boil and then add the stock.

6 Scrape up any juices stuck to the tin with a wooden spoon or spatula and boil rapidly for a few minutes until reduced a little. Strain the gravy into a jug and serve with three skinless slices of chicken per person, garnished with the roasted lemon wedges and the roast potatoes.

Cheesy turkey meatloaf

Serves 4

340 calories per serving

Takes 10 minutes to prepare,
    30 minutes to cook

2 medium slices white bread,
    torn roughly

1 onion, chopped roughly

1 courgette, grated coarsely

500 g (1 lb 2 oz) minced
    turkey

1 tablespoon fresh thyme
    leaves, plus extra to garnish

2 tablespoons tomato ketchup

75 g (2¾ oz) half fat mature
    Cheddar cheese, grated

300 g (10½ oz) cherry
    tomatoes on the vine

salt and freshly ground black
    pepper

*This meatloaf is delicious served with runner beans
and mashed potato (200 g/7 oz potatoes, mashed with
2 tablespoons of skimmed milk per person).*

1 Preheat the oven to Gas Mark 6/200°C/fan oven 180°C.
Place the bread and onion in a food processor and whizz until
finely chopped. Tip into a mixing bowl.

2 Squeeze the excess liquid from the courgette and add to
the bowl, along with the turkey, thyme, ketchup and half the
cheese. Season and mix well. Shape the mixture into a loaf
around 8 x 20 cm (3¼ x 8 inches) and place in a non stick
roasting tin. Bake in the oven for 20 minutes.

3 Snip the vine tomatoes into small clusters and arrange
around the meatloaf. Baste with the juices in the tin. Cook for
5 minutes and then scatter the remaining cheese over the
meatloaf. Cook for a final 5 minutes.

4 Slice the meatloaf and serve with the roasted tomatoes
and a sprinkling of fresh thyme leaves.

Chicken biryani

Serves 4

395 calories per serving

Takes 10 minutes to prepare,
  30 minutes to cook

❄

1 tablespoon vegetable oil

2 garlic cloves, crushed

2 teaspoons finely grated
  fresh root ginger

1 large onion, chopped

350 g (12 oz) skinless
  boneless chicken breasts,
  cut into chunks

½ teaspoon ground cinnamon

2 teaspoons ground coriander

1 teaspoon ground cumin

½ teaspoon turmeric

225 g (8 oz) dried long grain
  rice

900 ml (1½ pints) hot chicken
  stock

4 tomatoes, cut into quarters

salt and freshly ground black
  pepper

To serve

4 tablespoons low fat natural
  yogurt

a handful of chopped fresh
  coriander

Chicken, spices and long grain rice make a quick and tasty Indian-inspired dish.

1 Heat the oil in a large non stick frying pan. Add the garlic, ginger and onion and sauté gently for 2 minutes.

2 Add the chicken and cook for another 3–4 minutes, until browned. Stir in the cinnamon, coriander, cumin, turmeric and rice. Cook, stirring, for 1–2 minutes.

3 Pour in the stock and add the tomatoes. Cook over a low heat, stirring occasionally, until the liquid has been absorbed and the rice is tender. If the rice is not tender when all the liquid has evaporated, add a little extra stock or water and cook for a few more minutes.

4 Season to taste and serve, garnished with the yogurt and coriander.

Ⓥ **Variation...** For a vegetarian version, make this recipe with 350 g (12 oz) Quorn Chicken Style Pieces instead of chicken and use vegetable stock.

Tzatziki turkey burgers

Serves 4
185 calories per serving
Takes 30 minutes
❄ (uncooked burgers)

**calorie controlled cooking
  spray**
1 onion, chopped finely
2 garlic cloves, crushed
450 g (1 lb) minced turkey
**1 small red chilli, de-seeded
  and chopped finely**
a dash of Tabasco sauce
1 tablespoon soy sauce
**a small bunch of fresh
  coriander, chopped**
**salt and freshly ground black
  pepper**

For the sauce
**½ cucumber, halved
  lengthways, de-seeded and
  diced finely**
**150 g (5½ oz) 0% fat Greek
  yogurt**
**a small handful of fresh mint,
  chopped**

*Turkey combined with chilli and fresh coriander makes
these burgers very tasty. Serve with crisp lettuce, tomatoes
and the minty yogurt sauce.*

1 Spray a non stick frying pan with the cooking spray and fry
the onion and garlic for about 5 minutes, until softened and
golden, adding a splash of water if necessary to prevent them
from sticking.

2 Place the minced turkey in a bowl and add the fried onion
and garlic, chilli, Tabasco sauce, soy sauce, coriander and
seasoning. Using wet hands, shape into eight large patties.
Preheat the grill or heat a non stick griddle pan.

3 Grill the burgers on a foil-lined grill pan or hot griddle pan
for about 5 minutes on each side or until cooked through and
golden brown.

4 Meanwhile, make the sauce by mixing together the
cucumber, yogurt, mint and seasoning. Serve the burgers with
the sauce.

Creamy chicken bake

Serves 4

340 calories per serving

Takes 10 minutes to prepare,
45 minutes to cook

**calorie controlled cooking
spray**

**300 g (10½ oz) skinless
boneless chicken breasts,
diced**

2 small courgettes, sliced

175 g (6 oz) dried fusilli

**600 g (1 lb 5 oz) passata with
herbs**

**200 g (7 oz) low fat soft
cheese with garlic and herbs**

Creamy chicken pasta goes down a treat with everyone.

1 Preheat the oven to Gas Mark 5/190°C/fan oven 170°C. Heat
a non stick frying pan until hot and then spray with the cooking
spray. Add the chicken pieces and courgettes and stir-fry for
3–5 minutes until browned all over.

2 Meanwhile, bring a pan of water to the boil, add the pasta
and cook for 2 minutes only. Drain.

3 Add the passata and 100 ml (3½ fl oz) of water to the
chicken and courgettes and stir in. Bring to the boil.

4 Remove from the heat and stir in the pasta and soft cheese.
Pour into an ovenproof baking dish, cover with foil and bake for
45 minutes until the chicken and pasta are cooked.

Thai chicken curry

Serves 4
230 calories per serving
Takes 20 minutes

A delicious Thai curry, highly flavoured and hot. Serve with 60 g (2 oz) dried basmati rice per person, cooked according to the packet instructions, and steamed green beans, broccoli or pak choi, sprinkled with soy sauce.

calorie controlled cooking spray
2 garlic cloves, crushed
2 onions, chopped
2.5 cm (1 inch) fresh root ginger, chopped finely
4 x 165 g (5¾ oz) skinless boneless chicken breasts, cut into bite size pieces
1–2 teaspoons Thai green or red curry paste
3 tablespoons soy sauce
grated zest and juice of a lime
125 ml (4 fl oz) chicken stock
½ teaspoon caster sugar
100 g (3½ oz) watercress
a small bunch of fresh coriander, chopped roughly
1 tablespoon peanuts, toasted and chopped, to garnish

1 Heat a wok or large non stick frying pan on a high heat, spray with the cooking spray and fry the garlic, onions and ginger quickly, until golden brown, adding a little water if necessary to prevent them from sticking.

2 Add the chicken pieces and brown them all over. Add the curry paste and stir until the chicken is coated. Add the soy sauce, lime zest and juice, stock and sugar and cook for a further 2 minutes.

3 Add the watercress and coriander, reserving a little coriander to garnish, and cook for another 2 minutes. If the mixture begins to dry out, add a little more water, although the curry is meant to be quite dry.

4 Serve garnished with the peanuts and reserved coriander.

Monday's pie

Serves 4

465 calories per serving

Takes 25 minutes to prepare, 20 minutes to cook

❄

calorie controlled cooking spray

125 g (4½ oz) mushrooms, sliced

25 g (1 oz) sauce flour or cornflour

250 ml (9 fl oz) skimmed milk

150 ml (5 fl oz) chicken stock

225 g (8 oz) cooked skinless chicken breast, diced

1 tablespoon chopped fresh parsley

1 teaspoon lemon juice

salt and freshly ground black pepper

For the pastry

225 g (8 oz) plain white flour, plus extra for rolling

2 teaspoons baking powder

75 g (2¾ oz) low fat spread

1 tablespoon chopped fresh parsley

This is the perfect way to serve leftovers from a roast chicken or turkey. It makes a delicious and filling meal when served with lots of steamed vegetables.

1 Preheat the oven to Gas Mark 7/220°C/fan oven 200°C.

2 Spray a large non stick saucepan with the cooking spray. Add the mushrooms and cook them for 3–4 minutes, stirring often.

3 Blend the sauce flour or cornflour with the milk and pour into the saucepan with the stock. Heat gently, stirring constantly, until thickened. Add the chicken, parsley and lemon juice and season.

4 Sift the flour and baking powder into a mixing bowl with a pinch of salt. Rub in the low fat spread using your fingertips until the mixture resembles fine breadcrumbs. Stir in the parsley and add sufficient cold water to make a soft, but not sticky, dough. Roll out the dough on a lightly floured surface to a thickness of about 8 mm (⅜ inch).

5 Transfer the chicken mixture to an ovenproof baking dish and top with the pastry crust. Bake for about 20 minutes until browned.

🕑 **Variation...** For a vegetarian version, substitute Quorn Chicken Style Pieces for the chicken and use vegetable stock.

Creamy pesto pasta

Serves 4
505 calories per serving
Takes 20 minutes

**250 g (9 oz) dried trofie pasta
or other small pasta shapes**

**calorie controlled cooking
spray**

**500 g (1 lb 2 oz) skinless
boneless turkey steaks, cut
into short strips**

2 garlic cloves, sliced

5 spring onions, sliced finely

2 tablespoons fresh red pesto

**150 g (5½ oz) half fat crème
fraîche**

**75 g (2¾ oz) mild or hot
pepperdew peppers in brine,
drained and sliced finely**

150 ml (5 fl oz) chicken stock

**salt and freshly ground black
pepper**

*Why spend time and money at an Italian restaurant when
you can cook something so simple, and just as tasty, at
home? If you can't find fresh pesto, use 2 tablespoons of
red pesto from a jar.*

1 Bring a large pan of water to the boil, add the pasta and
cook according to the packet instructions until al dente.

2 Meanwhile, heat a wide non stick saucepan and spray with
the cooking spray. Add the turkey and cook for 5 minutes,
stirring until brown all over. You may have to do this in batches.
Return all the turkey to the pan, add the garlic and spring
onions and cook for a further 3 minutes.

3 Add the pesto, crème fraîche, peppers and stock. Bring just
to the boil and check the seasoning. Drain the pasta and stir
through the sauce. Serve immediately.

⊘ **Variation...** For a vegetarian version, use a 350 g packet
of Quorn Chicken Style Pieces, instead of the turkey, and
vegetable stock.

Lemon chicken

Serves 4

265 calories per serving

Takes 12 minutes to prepare +
20 minutes chilling,
20 minutes to cook

❄ (for up to 1 month)

**2 x 165 g (5¾ oz) skinless
boneless chicken breasts,
cut into thin strips**

1 egg white, beaten

2½ teaspoons cornflour

65 ml (2½ fl oz) chicken stock

3 tablespoons lemon juice

1 teaspoon artificial sweetener

1 tablespoon soy sauce

2 garlic cloves, crushed

½ teaspoon dried chilli flakes

**calorie controlled cooking
spray**

2 leeks, sliced

**150 g (5½ oz) dried basmati
rice**

1 teaspoon sesame oil

2 spring onions, chopped

*A delicate chicken recipe, with a little spice and a hint
of lemon.*

1 In a large bowl, mix together the chicken strips, egg white
and 1½ teaspoons of cornflour. Set aside to chill in the fridge
for 20 minutes.

2 Bring a pan of water to the boil and drop in the chicken
strips. Cook for 1–2 minutes until the chicken turns completely
white. Drain and set aside.

3 In a wok or large non stick frying pan, mix together the
chicken stock, lemon juice, sweetener, soy sauce, garlic and
chilli flakes. Blend the remaining teaspoon of cornflour with a
teaspoon of water to a paste and mix the paste into the sauce.
Bring to the boil and, when the mixture starts to thicken, add
the chicken and cook for 6–8 minutes, stirring occasionally.

4 Meanwhile, spray another non stick pan with the cooking
spray and fry the leeks for 3–4 minutes. Stir in the rice and
pour in enough water to cover. Bring to the boil and simmer for
8–10 minutes, until the rice is cooked.

5 Pour the sesame oil into the chicken mixture and sprinkle
with the spring onions.

6 Drain the rice and leeks and divide between four plates.
Spoon over the chicken and serve immediately.

Teriyaki turkey noodles

Serves 4
440 calories per serving
Takes 25 minutes
❄

250 g (9 oz) dried medium egg
   noodles
600 ml (20 fl oz) boiling
   chicken stock
3 tablespoons teriyaki sauce
1 tablespoon vegetable oil
450 g (1 lb) skinless boneless
   turkey breast, cut into thin
   strips
175 g (6 oz) carrots, peeled
   and cut into matchsticks
100 g (3½ oz) celery stick,
   sliced thinly
125 g (4½ oz) mange tout
a bunch of spring onions,
   shredded
2 tablespoons tomato ketchup
2 teaspoons cornflour
2 tablespoons sherry

A simple stir-fry packed full of flavour.

1 Place the noodles in a bowl, pour over the boiling stock, stir in the teriyaki sauce and leave for 15 minutes.

2 Meanwhile, heat the oil in a wok or large non stick frying pan and add the turkey strips. Stir-fry for 5 minutes and then add the carrots, celery and mange tout. Stir-fry for a further 5 minutes.

3 Drain the noodles, reserving the liquid, and add them to the wok or pan with the spring onions, mixing well. Add the reserved liquid and bring to the boil.

4 Mix together the tomato ketchup, cornflour and sherry and add this to the pan. Cook, stirring, until the sauce thickens a little and then serve at once.

Basque chicken casserole

Serves 4

265 calories per serving

Takes 25 minutes to prepare,
  1 hour to cook

❄

**calorie controlled cooking
  spray**

**4 x 175 g (6 oz) skinless
  boneless chicken breasts**

**225 g (8 oz) shallots, peeled
  but left whole**

2 garlic cloves, crushed

400 g can chopped tomatoes

½ teaspoon paprika

**2 red, yellow or orange
  peppers, de-seeded and
  chopped**

2 bay leaves

150 ml (5 fl oz) dry white wine

**salt and freshly ground black
  pepper**

To serve

1 tablespoon capers

grated zest of a lemon

**a small bunch of fresh basil,
  chopped**

**1 small red chilli, de-seeded
  and chopped finely (optional)**

*Most of the cooking for this delicious dish is done in the
oven without you having to worry about it.*

1 Preheat the oven to Gas Mark 2/150°C/fan oven 130°C. Heat
a large non stick frying pan and spray with the cooking spray.
Fry the chicken breasts for 5–6 minutes until golden. Season
and set aside.

2 At the same time, heat a large, lidded, flame and ovenproof
casserole dish, spray with the cooking spray and fry the
shallots and garlic for 4 minutes, until starting to brown. Add
a splash of water if necessary to prevent them from sticking.

3 Add the tomatoes, paprika, peppers, bay leaves, white
wine and seasoning and 100 ml (3½ fl oz) of water. Bring to
the boil, incorporate any browned juices from the base of the
pan and stir well. Add the browned chicken breasts, cover
and cook in the oven for 1 hour.

4 Remove from the oven, check the seasoning and sprinkle
with the capers, lemon zest, chopped basil and chilli, if using,
to serve.

Oriental chicken parcels

Serves 4

175 calories per serving

Takes 30 minutes to prepare,
25 minutes to cook

175 g (6 oz) dried basmati rice
calorie controlled cooking
spray
1 teaspoon sesame oil
4 spring onions, sliced
1 cm (½ inch) fresh root
ginger, grated
2 x 175 g (6 oz) skinless
boneless chicken breasts,
cut into 2 cm (¾ inch) cubes
100 g (3½ oz) shiitake
mushrooms, sliced
2 tablespoons soy sauce

Chicken breasts are steamed in baking paper with
mushrooms, rice and a light aromatic sauce of soy, fresh
ginger and spring onions.

1 Bring a pan of water to the boil, add the rice and cook
according to the packet instructions. Drain thoroughly and set
aside.

2 Heat a large non stick frying pan and spray with the cooking
spray. Add the sesame oil, spring onions and ginger and fry
for 1 minute. Add the chicken and mushrooms and stir-fry for
2 minutes more. Add the soy and cooked rice and cook for a
further minute.

3 Cut four pieces of baking paper approximately 15 cm
(6 inches) square and divide the mixture evenly between
them. Fold up the paper to enclose the filling, securing by
folding underneath.

4 Bring a pan of water to the boil and place the parcels in a
steamer over the boiling water. Steam for 25 minutes.

5 Serve, allowing each guest to open their own parcel.

Tip... Instead of using a steamer, you can use a colander
suspended over a pan of boiling water, using the pan lid to
cover the parcels.

Stuffed chicken breasts

Serves 4

212 calories per serving

Takes 20 minutes to prepare,
    20 minutes to cook

**100 g (3½ oz) low fat soft
    cheese**

**50 g (1¾ oz) wafer thin ham,
    chopped finely**

**50 g (1¾ oz) baby mushrooms,
    chopped finely**

**4 x 150 g (5½ oz) skinless
    boneless chicken breasts**

**salt and freshly ground black
    pepper**

*This recipe is just right for a delicious midweek dinner.
Serve with steamed carrots and a grated courgette gratin.
This is also good served cold with a salad.*

1 Preheat the oven to Gas Mark 4/180°C/fan oven 160°C.

2 In a small bowl, mix the soft cheese, ham and mushrooms
into a thick paste. Season.

3 Lay a chicken breast flat on a work surface, place your hand
flat on the top to hold it firm and, holding a sharp knife parallel
with the work surface, cut a slit in the side of the chicken
breast. Repeat with the remaining chicken breasts and divide
the soft cheese mixture between the four pockets.

4 Wrap each stuffed breast securely in a piece of foil. Place
in a shallow ovenproof dish or on a baking tray. Bake in the
oven for 20 minutes.

5 Check the chicken is cooked by opening a parcel and
piercing the chicken with a skewer. If the juices run clear, serve
immediately with the juices from the foil parcel poured over the
meat.

Tip... To serve, cut the chicken into slices to reveal the
stuffing inside.

Variation... If you prefer your meat browned, about
5 minutes before the chicken is ready, preheat the grill
to high. Leaving the chicken in the foil, but opening each
parcel up to make a bowl shape, spray the chicken with
calorie controlled cooking spray. Put the chicken breasts,
still in the foil, under the grill for 5 minutes or until
browned to your liking.

Turkey cannelloni

Serves 4

484 calories per serving

Takes 30 minutes to prepare +
20 minutes soaking,
45 minutes to cook

**250 g (9 oz) dried no-precook
cannelloni tubes**

**25 g packet fresh parsley,
chopped**

1 teaspoon paprika

**salt and freshly ground black
pepper**

For the filling

**15 g (½ oz) dried porcini
mushrooms**

150 ml (5 fl oz) boiling water

**calorie controlled cooking
spray**

450 g (1 lb) minced turkey

2 onions, diced finely

4 garlic cloves, crushed

**4 fresh thyme sprigs, chopped,
or 2 teaspoons dried thyme**

**1 tablespoon Worcestershire
sauce**

For the topping

2 teaspoons cornflour

**450 g (1 lb) low fat natural
yogurt**

**100 g (3½ oz) low fat soft
cheese**

*Make sure you buy the cannelloni that doesn't need any
precooking.*

1 Preheat the oven to Gas Mark 6/200°C/fan oven 180°C.

2 Place the porcini mushrooms in a jug, pour over the boiling
water and set aside for 20 minutes. Drain, reserving the
soaking liquid, and chop.

3 To make the filling, spray a large non stick frying pan with
the cooking spray and put over a medium heat. Add the minced
turkey, onions and garlic and season. Fry until the mince is
browned all over, breaking it up with a spoon.

4 Add the mushrooms and their soaking liquid, the thyme and
Worcestershire sauce. Cook for 15 minutes or until most of the
liquid has evaporated. Fill the cannelloni tubes with spoonfuls
of the mixture and lay in an ovenproof dish.

5 Blend the cornflour to a paste with 1 tablespoon of water
and mix with the yogurt. Add the soft cheese, season and pour
over the cannelloni.

6 Bake in the oven for 45 minutes. Before serving, sprinkle
with the parsley and paprika.

Tip... Porcini mushrooms are strongly flavoured Italian
mushrooms that can be bought dried. To use, soak them in
enough boiling water to cover them for about 20 minutes.
Use the soaking liquid as well as the mushrooms.

Fantastic fish and seafood

Fish and chips

Serves 4

400 calories per serving

Takes 15 minutes to prepare,
  50 minutes to cook

2 tablespoons olive oil

700 g (1 lb 9 oz) potatoes,
  scrubbed and cut into
  wedges

2 tablespoons plain white
  flour

1 egg

50 g (1¾ oz) dried white
  breadcrumbs

4 x 175 g (6 oz) skinless cod
  fillets

salt and freshly ground black
  pepper

malt vinegar or lemon wedges,
  to serve

*Instead of frying – which adds fat – try this oven-baked
version of one of Britain's best-loved dishes.*

1 Preheat the oven to Gas Mark 6/200°C/fan oven 180°C.
Grease a non stick roasting tin and non stick baking tray with
1 teaspoon of the oil. Heat the roasting tin in the oven for
5 minutes.

2 Put the potato wedges in the roasting tin and sprinkle them
with the remaining oil. Toss them together and then season.
Bake for about 30 minutes, until just tender.

3 Meanwhile, sprinkle the flour on a plate and season. Beat
the egg in a shallow bowl with 2 tablespoons of cold water and
sprinkle the breadcrumbs on a separate plate.

4 Rinse the fish fillets and pat them dry with kitchen towel.
Coat the fish fillets in the seasoned flour, dip the floured fish
fillets in the egg and then coat them in the breadcrumbs. Place
the fillets on the prepared baking tray.

5 Reduce the oven temperature to Gas Mark 5/190°C/fan
oven 170°C and continue to bake the potatoes, with the
fish positioned on the shelf below them, for a further
15–20 minutes. Check that the fish is cooked by testing it
with a fork – the flesh should be opaque and flake easily.

6 Serve the fish with the baked wedges, seasoned with malt
vinegar or with lemon wedges.

Variation... Try using coley or haddock instead of cod.

Chunky fish fingers

Serves 4
260 calories per serving
Takes 35 minutes
❄ (fish fingers only)

8 x 15 g (½ oz) wholewheat crispbreads
4 x 100 g (3½ oz) skinless cod loin fillets, each cut into 2 or 3 long fingers
1 egg, beaten
250 g (9 oz) frozen peas
½ x 25 g packet fresh mint, leaves only

For the tartare sauce
juice of ½ a lemon
4 tablespoons Quark
1 tablespoon low fat natural yogurt
1 tablespoon chopped fresh dill
1 teaspoon capers, drained and chopped finely
25 g (1 oz) cocktail gherkins, chopped finely

Serve with tomato halves, grilled under a hot grill for a few minutes, carrots and sweetcorn.

1 Put the wholewheat crispbreads into a food processor and whizz until fine crumbs form, or use a hand blender. Transfer to a shallow dish. Dip the cod pieces in the wholewheat crumbs, coating them thoroughly. Dip the cod pieces into the beaten egg and then back into the crumbs, ensuring they are completely coated.

2 Preheat the grill to medium high and grill the fish fingers for 10 minutes, turning once halfway through.

3 Meanwhile, bring a pan of water to the boil, add the peas and bring to the boil. Simmer for 3 minutes or until tender. Drain the peas and then whizz them briefly in a food processor with the mint leaves, until half puréed. Keep warm.

4 Mix together all the ingredients for the tartare sauce in a bowl and serve with the fish fingers and mushy peas.

Pizza marinara

Serves 4

266 calories per serving

Takes 20 minutes to prepare
 + proving, 12–15 minutes
 to cook

For the pizza base

**140 g (5 oz) strong white flour,
 2 teaspoons reserved for
 dusting**

½ teaspoon instant dried yeast

a pinch of salt

For the topping

**calorie controlled cooking
 spray**

1 onion, sliced thinly

1 garlic clove, crushed

400 g can chopped tomatoes

1 tablespoon tomato purée

2 teaspoons dried mixed herbs

**200 g (7 oz) cooked peeled
 prawns, defrosted if frozen**

**185 g can tuna in brine or
 spring water, drained**

**50 g (1¾ oz) half fat Cheddar
 cheese, grated**

**salt and freshly ground black
 pepper**

**25 g (1 oz) capers, to serve
 (optional)**

A tasty pizza topped with prawns and tuna.

1 Place the flour in a large bowl and stir in the yeast and salt. Add 7–8 tablespoons of hand hot water and mix in. It's easiest to do this with a wooden spoon to start with and then use your hands.

2 Sprinkle the reserved flour on to a clean work surface. Once the dough has come together and no longer clings to the sides of the bowl, turn it out on to the lightly floured surface. Knead the dough for at least 5 minutes until it is soft and stretchy. Roll out the dough to a 24 cm (9½ inch) circle.

3 Spray a non stick baking tray with the cooking spray. Place the dough on the tray and cover it with a clean cloth. Leave in a warm, draught free place to prove until doubled in size, about 20–30 minutes or a little longer if not yet doubled after this time. Preheat the oven to Gas Mark 7/220°C/fan oven 200°C.

4 Spray a saucepan with the cooking spray and heat until sizzling. Add the onion and cook over a medium heat for 5 minutes until softened, adding a splash of water if necessary to prevent it from sticking. Add the garlic and tomatoes and simmer for 5 minutes. Stir in the tomato purée, herbs and seasoning.

5 Spread the sauce over the pizza base, top with the prawns and tuna and sprinkle with the cheese. Bake for 12–15 minutes until golden. Top with the capers to serve, if using.

Tuna and sweetcorn rosti cake

Serves 4
294 calories per serving
Takes 45 minutes

750 g (1 lb 10 oz) floury or
    waxy potatoes, unpeeled and
    left whole
calorie controlled cooking
    spray
1 large onion, sliced thinly
150 g (5½ oz) frozen
    sweetcorn
½ a kettleful of boiling water
2 x 200 g cans tuna in spring
    water, drained
1 tablespoon sunflower oil
salt and freshly ground black
    pepper

*Don't worry if the rosti breaks up a little when you turn it
over – it will still taste good.*

1 Bring a lidded pan of water to the boil and add the
potatoes. Cover and cook for 12 minutes. Drain, cover with
cold water and set aside to cool for 2 minutes. Drain again
and, when cool enough to handle, scrape off the skins using a
table knife. Coarsely grate the potatoes into a bowl.

2 Meanwhile, spray a lidded non stick frying pan with the
cooking spray and cook the onion for 3–4 minutes until
starting to colour. Add 6 tablespoons of water to the pan.
Cover and cook gently for 5 minutes until the onions are
softened and the liquid has evaporated.

3 Place the sweetcorn in a bowl, cover with boiling water and
leave to defrost for 2 minutes. Drain.

4 Using a couple of forks, mix the onion, sweetcorn and tuna
into the grated potato. Heat half the oil in a non stick frying pan
and then add the rosti mixture to make one large rosti, pressing
down firmly. Cook for 7 minutes over a medium heat.

5 Upturn the rosti on to a plate. Add the remaining oil to the
frying pan. Slide the rosti back into the frying pan to cook
the other side for a further 7 minutes. Cut into four wedges
and serve.

Variation... Try replacing the tuna with a 418 g drained can
of red salmon.

Seafood and parsley tart

Serves 4

347 calories per serving

Takes 35 minutes to prepare +
30 minutes chilling,
30–35 minutes to bake

For the pastry

50 g (1¾ oz) low fat spread

**100 g (3½ oz) plain white flour,
plus extra for dusting**

1 egg white, beaten

For the filling

**calorie controlled cooking
spray**

4 shallots, chopped

4 garlic cloves, chopped

**500 g (1 lb 2 oz) seafood
selection, defrosted if frozen**

50 ml (2 fl oz) dry white wine

**a small bunch of fresh parsley,
chopped**

2 eggs, beaten

150 ml (5 fl oz) skimmed milk

**salt and freshly ground black
pepper**

*A ready-mixed seafood selection makes this tart so simple
to put together.*

1 Make the pastry by rubbing the low fat spread into the
flour until the mixture resembles fresh breadcrumbs. Add
1 tablespoon of cold water and mould into a ball with your
hands. Wrap in cling film and chill for 30 minutes. Preheat the
oven to Gas Mark 6/200°C/fan oven 180°C.

2 Roll out the pastry on a floured surface to a circle about
5 mm (¼ inch) thick and use to line a 19 cm (7½ inch) diameter
loose-bottomed flan tin. Line with foil or non stick baking
parchment and fill with baking beans. Bake blind for 15 minutes.

3 Remove the beans and lining, brush the pastry case with
the egg white and bake for 5–10 minutes until golden.

4 Lower the oven temperature to Gas Mark 5/190°C/fan oven
170°C and spray a non stick pan with the cooking spray. Fry
the shallots and garlic for about 5 minutes until softened,
adding a splash of water if necessary to prevent them from
sticking. Add the seafood, white wine and parsley and heat
through.

5 In a large bowl, beat the eggs, milk and seasoning
together. Add the seafood mixture and pour into the pastry
case. Bake for 30–35 minutes, until set and lightly browned.

Traditional fishcakes

Serves 4
200 calories per serving
Takes 45 minutes
❊ (before cooking)

300 g (10½ oz) potatoes,
  peeled and chopped roughly
3 leeks, chopped finely
4 x 150 g (5½ oz) skinless cod
  fillets
1 teaspoon French mustard
a small bunch of fresh parsley
  or dill
1 tablespoon virtually fat free
  plain fromage frais
salt and freshly ground black
  pepper

*Home-made fishcakes are a world away from the
shop-bought variety – and children love them. Serve with
steamed mange tout.*

1 Bring a pan of water to the boil, add the potatoes and cook
for 20 minutes, or until tender. Drain and mash. At the same
time, steam the leeks in a covered colander or sieve over the
potatoes until tender. Preheat the grill.

2 Grill the fish for about 5 minutes, until cooked through, and
then flake into a bowl, removing any bones.

3 Add the mash, leeks, mustard, herbs, fromage frais and
seasoning to the fish and gently fold together. Using wet hands,
shape into eight patties.

4 Grill for 3–4 minutes on each side, or until golden brown,
crunchy and hot right through. Serve.

Spicy seafood and tomato pasta

Serves 4

485 calories per serving

Takes 10 minutes to prepare,
  25 minutes to cook

**calorie controlled cooking
  spray**

2 onions, chopped

2 garlic cloves, chopped finely

**1 red chilli, de-seeded and
  chopped finely**

**400 g (14 oz) seafood
  selection, defrosted if frozen**

2 tablespoons dry white wine

**2 x 400 g cans chopped
  tomatoes**

**2 tablespoons Worcestershire
  sauce**

1 teaspoon caster sugar

350 g (12 oz) dried spaghetti

**salt and freshly ground black
  pepper**

**25 g packet fresh basil,
  chopped, to serve**

*This seafood sauce can be cooked in a flash. If you're
using fresh seafood, a mixture of prawns, mussels, squid
and cockles is good.*

1 Spray a wok or large non stick frying pan with the cooking
spray and put over a medium heat. Stir-fry the onions, garlic
and chilli for 5 minutes or until the onions are soft.

2 Add the seafood, white wine, tomatoes, Worcestershire sauce,
sugar and seasoning and cook for 25 minutes or until the sauce
is reduced and thick.

3 Meanwhile, bring a pan of water to the boil, add the pasta
and cook according to the packet instructions. Drain.

4 Toss the sauce with the pasta and check the seasoning.
Sprinkle with the basil and serve.

Fish pie

Serves 4

423 calories per serving

Takes 30 minutes to prepare, 25 minutes to cook

❄ (before cooking)

500 g (1 lb 2 oz) smoked haddock fillets

600 ml (20 fl oz) skimmed milk

2 bay leaves

750 g (1 lb 10 oz) potatoes, all roughly the same size, scrubbed

300 g (10½ oz) cooked peeled prawns, defrosted if frozen

40 g (1½ oz) low fat spread

50 g (1¾ oz) plain white flour

1 tablespoon lemon juice

1 tablespoon chopped fresh parsley

salt and freshly ground black pepper

This fish pie has a rosti-style grated potato topping instead of the usual mash.

1 Preheat the oven to Gas Mark 4/180°C/fan oven 160°C.

2 Place the haddock in a roasting tin, pour in the milk, add the bay leaves and bake in the oven for 15 minutes or until the fish flakes easily.

3 Meanwhile, bring a pan of water to the boil, add the unpeeled potatoes and cook for 8 minutes. Drain and leave to cool slightly.

4 Lift the fish on to a plate, reserving the milk, and break into flakes using a fork, discarding any skin and bones. Transfer to an ovenproof baking dish and mix with the prawns.

5 Place the low fat spread and flour in a non stick saucepan and gradually blend in the reserved fishy milk. Bring to a simmer, stirring until smooth, and simmer for 3 minutes. Add the lemon juice, parsley and seasoning to taste. Remove the bay leaves and pour into the baking dish.

6 Scrape the skins from the potatoes and then coarsely grate the potatoes straight over the baking dish to form an even topping. Bake for 25 minutes until crisp and golden.

Italian fish stew

Serves 4
180 calories per serving
Takes 15 minutes to prepare
+ 30 minutes soaking,
30 minutes to cook

a pinch of saffron strands
2 tablespoons boiling water
calorie controlled cooking
**   spray**
1 large onion, chopped finely
2 garlic cloves, crushed
2 red peppers in brine, drained
**   and chopped**
2 x 400 g cans chopped
**   tomatoes**
300 ml (10 fl oz) vegetable
**   stock**
2 bay leaves
a small bunch of fresh basil,
**   chopped**
½ teaspoon Tabasco sauce
1 tablespoon tomato purée
450 g (1 lb) skinless cod
**   fillets, cut into bite size**
**   chunks**
8 large, cooked, shelled
**   prawns, defrosted if frozen**
salt and freshly ground black
**   pepper**

This is great to make in the summer. Try it served with
steamed green beans.

1 Place the saffron strands in the boiling water to soak for
30 minutes.

2 Heat a large, lidded, non stick saucepan and spray with
the cooking spray. Stir-fry the onion and garlic for 5 minutes
or until the onions have softened, adding a splash of water if
necessary to prevent them from sticking.

3 Stir in the peppers and tomatoes and add the stock, saffron
strands with their soaking liquid, bay leaves, half the basil, the
Tabasco sauce, tomato purée and seasoning. Bring to the boil
and then simmer for 20 minutes.

4 Add the cod and cook, covered, for a further 5 minutes.
Gently fold in the prawns and allow them to heat through.
Check the seasoning and scatter with the remaining basil to
serve.

Prawn stir-fry

Serves 4
208 calories per serving
Takes 15 minutes

125 g (4½ oz) dried rice noodles
calorie controlled cooking spray
1 large garlic clove, crushed
200 g (7 oz) large, cooked, peeled prawns, defrosted if frozen
2 tablespoons soy sauce
1 teaspoon caster sugar
juice of a lime
100 g (3½ oz) beansprouts
75 g (2¾ oz) radishes, chopped
2 carrots, peeled and cut into matchsticks
20 g (¾ oz) peanuts, chopped

To garnish
2 shallots, chopped finely
a small bunch of fresh coriander, chopped
1 teaspoon dried chilli flakes

A very quick recipe that is satisfying and full of robust flavours.

1 Bring a pan of water to the boil, add the noodles and cook for 5 minutes or according to the packet instructions.

2 Meanwhile, heat a wok or large non stick frying pan, spray with the cooking spray and stir-fry the garlic for a couple of minutes until golden brown. Add a splash of water if necessary to prevent it from sticking.

3 Add the prawns and stir-fry for a further 2 minutes. Stir in the soy sauce, sugar and lime juice.

4 Drain the noodles and snip into smaller lengths with scissors. Toss together with the beansprouts, radishes, carrots and peanuts in the pan. Stir-fry for a final 2 minutes and then serve immediately, garnished with the shallots, coriander and chilli flakes.

Cod and leek parcels

Serves 4

140 calories per serving

Takes 15 minutes to prepare,
20 minutes to cook

**4 x 125 g (4½ oz) skinless cod
fillets**

**2 leeks, halved lengthways
and sliced**

**grated zest and juice of a
lemon**

2 teaspoons olive oil

**salt and freshly ground black
pepper**

*Serve with 200 g (7 oz) cooked new potatoes per person,
for a fresh tasting quick supper.*

1 Preheat the oven to Gas Mark 4/180°C/fan oven 160°C.
Cut four pieces of non stick baking parchment about 30 cm
(12 inches) square and place a piece of fish in the centre of
each.

2 Share the other ingredients between the four fillets so that
each is evenly covered with leeks, lemon zest, lemon juice,
seasoning and a dribble of oil.

3 Scrunch up the baking parchment to make sealed parcels
and place on a baking tray. Bake for 20 minutes and serve in
the paper for each person to open their own parcel.

Variation... Try salmon, haddock or coley instead of the cod.

Salmon steaks in foil

Serves 4

335 calories per serving

Takes 10 minutes to prepare
+ marinating, 20 minutes
to cook

4 x 175 g (6 oz) salmon steaks
calorie controlled cooking
spray
4 teaspoons low fat spread
juice of 2 lemons
a small bunch of fresh parsley,
chopped
a small bunch of fresh dill,
chopped
salt and freshly ground black
pepper

To serve
2 tablespoons half fat crème
fraîche
4 fresh parsley or dill sprigs

Salmon steaks can be cooked with almost any combination
of your favourite herbs to create your own version of this
recipe. Serve with steamed green beans.

1 Spray four individual pieces of cooking foil, big enough to
enclose the fish entirely, with the cooking spray. Place a salmon
steak on each piece of foil. Put a teaspoon of low fat spread on
the top of each steak and then divide the rest of the ingredients
evenly between the parcels.

2 Fold up the foil to make sealed parcels and then leave in
the fridge to marinate for up to 3 hours but for a minimum of
10 minutes.

3 Preheat the oven to Gas Mark 6/200°C/fan oven 180°C and
bake the fish for 20 minutes, until cooked through.

4 To serve, open the foil and remove the fish on to plates,
reserving the juices in the foil. Remove the outer skin and the
central bone from the fish and pour over the juices left in the
foil. Top each steak with a little crème fraîche and garnish with
the herbs.

Variation... This recipe works equally well with cod steaks.

Thai noodles with crab meat

Serves 4
330 calories per serving
Takes 25 minutes

2 tablespoons fish sauce
1 tablespoon tomato purée
1 tablespoon rice wine vinegar
  or white wine vinegar
1 tablespoon demerara sugar
1 tablespoon lime juice
1 teaspoon cornflour
1 garlic clove, crushed
225 g (8 oz) dried flat rice
  noodles
a kettleful of boiling water
1 tablespoon sunflower oil
100 g (3½ oz) white cabbage,
  shredded
6 spring onions, sliced
1 carrot, peeled and grated
100 g (3½ oz) beansprouts
1 teaspoon dried chilli flakes
200 g (7 oz) canned white crab
  meat, drained
2 tablespoons chopped fresh
  coriander

Pad Thai is usually served with prawns or chicken. In this version, crab meat is used for a change.

1 Mix together the fish sauce, tomato purée, vinegar, sugar, lime juice, cornflour and garlic and set aside.

2 Place the rice noodles in a bowl and cover with boiling water. Leave to soak for 10 minutes. Drain thoroughly.

3 Meanwhile, heat the oil in a wok or large non stick pan and add the cabbage, spring onions, carrot, beansprouts and chilli flakes. Stir-fry for 2–3 minutes until beginning to soften and then add the noodles. Stir-fry for a further 5 minutes.

4 Mix the crab meat with the coriander and prepared sauce and add to the pan. Toss well and heat through for a further 2–3 minutes.

Variation... If you wish, you could garnish this dish with 15 g (½ oz) chopped, salted peanuts.

Roasted tomato cod with parsley mash

Serves 4
300 calories per serving
Takes 35 minutes
❄

For the mash

700 g (1 lb 9 oz) potatoes, peeled and diced

3 tablespoons virtually fat free plain fromage frais

2 tablespoons chopped fresh parsley

salt and freshly ground black pepper

For the fish

4 x 150 g (5½ oz) skinless cod fillets

2 tablespoons sun-dried tomato purée

1 tomato, de-seeded and chopped finely

25 g (1 oz) stoned black olives in brine, drained and chopped finely

salt and freshly ground black pepper

Tasty comfort food; perfect for a wintry evening.

1 Preheat the oven to Gas Mark 5/190°C/fan oven 170°C.

2 Bring a pan of water to the boil, add the potatoes and cook for 15 minutes until tender. Drain thoroughly and mash with the fromage frais, parsley and seasoning. Cover and keep warm.

3 Meanwhile, place the cod fillets in a non stick roasting tin. Mix together the tomato purée, chopped tomato and olives. Spread this mixture over the top of each cod fillet and bake for 15 minutes.

4 Spoon a little of the mash on to four serving plates and top each with a cooked cod fillet. Season and serve.

Variation... Flavour your mash with other ingredients, such as crushed garlic, a teaspoon of wholegrain mustard or toasted cumin seeds. Adding any fresh herbs also gives it that little extra flavour.

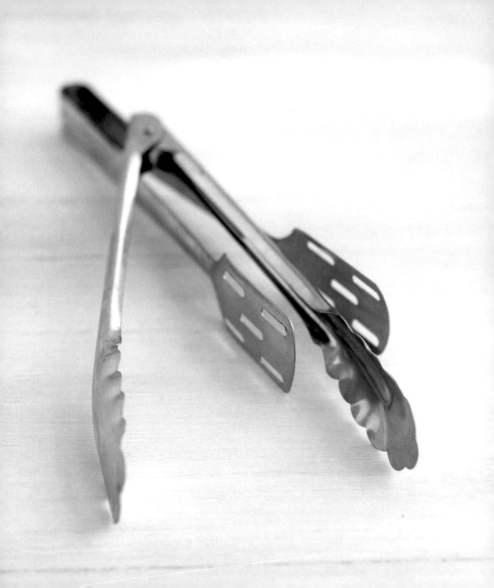

Simply vegetarian

One pot veggie curry

Serves 4

253 calories per serving

Takes 15 minutes to prepare,
20 minutes to cook

Ⓥ

*This delicious curry is crammed full of multicoloured
vegetables. Any leftover curry is wonderful spooned over a
225 g (8 oz) potato per person, baked in its skin.*

**calorie controlled cooking
spray**

1 onion, chopped roughly

**1 red pepper, de-seeded and
chopped roughly**

**1 yellow pepper, de-seeded
and chopped roughly**

**2 teaspoons grated fresh root
ginger**

2 garlic cloves, crushed

**1 tablespoon medium curry
powder**

**500 g (1 lb 2 oz) potatoes,
peeled and diced**

225 g (8 oz) cauliflower florets

**850 ml (1½ pints) vegetable
stock**

110 g (4 oz) dried red lentils

**150 g (5½ oz) green beans, cut
into thirds**

**salt and freshly ground black
pepper**

**a handful of chopped fresh
coriander, to serve**

1 Heat a large, lidded, non stick saucepan or flameproof
casserole dish, spray with the cooking spray and brown the
onion for 2 minutes. Tip the peppers into the pan and stir-fry
for a further 2 minutes. Stir in the ginger, garlic and curry
powder and cook for 30 seconds.

2 Add the potatoes and cauliflower to the pan and stir to coat
in the spice mixture. Pour in the vegetable stock and lentils,
mix together well and season lightly. Bring the mixture to a
simmer, cover the pan and cook for 10 minutes.

3 Stir the green beans into the curry, replace the lid and cook
gently for a further 10 minutes or until the lentils have broken
down to thicken the sauce and the vegetables are tender.
Scatter with the coriander before serving.

Vegetable and lentil moussaka

Serves 4
205 calories per serving
Takes 45 minutes to prepare, 30 minutes to cook ✔ ❄

This is very filling – freeze what you don't need in small quantities ready for future use.

2 tablespoons dried green lentils
1 large aubergine, sliced into 5 mm (¼ inch) slices
2 teaspoons olive oil
1 large onion, chopped
1 garlic clove, crushed
3 carrots, peeled and sliced thinly
2 celery sticks, sliced thinly
100 g (3½ oz) mushrooms, sliced
3 tomatoes, skinned and chopped
1 courgette, sliced
300 ml (10 fl oz) vegetable stock

1 tablespoon tomato purée
a small bunch of fresh thyme, chopped
a small bunch of fresh basil, chopped
25 g (1 oz) half fat Cheddar cheese, grated
salt and freshly ground black pepper

For the onion and chive sauce
425 ml (15 fl oz) skimmed milk
1 small onion, chopped finely
a small bunch of fresh chives, chopped finely
2 tablespoons plain white flour
a pinch of grated nutmeg

1 Bring a pan of water to the boil, add the lentils, turn down the heat and simmer for 15 minutes, until the lentils are tender. Skim off any scum that comes to the surface. Drain and set aside.

2 Meanwhile, preheat the grill. Lay the slices of the aubergine on the grill pan, season and grill for about 10 minutes on each side, until dried out and golden.

3 Heat the oil in a large non stick frying pan and fry the onion and garlic for 5 minutes, until softened. Add the carrots, celery, mushrooms, tomatoes and courgette and stir-fry on a high heat for 2 minutes.

continues overleaf ▶

4 Add the cooked lentils, stock, tomato purée, thyme, basil and seasoning. Bring to the boil, turn down the heat and simmer for 10 minutes until the mixture is slightly reduced and thickened.

5 Meanwhile, make the onion and chive sauce. Place all but 4 tablespoons of the milk in a small saucepan with the onion and chives and bring to the boil. In a small bowl, mix the remaining cold milk with the flour to make a smooth paste. Add the paste to the hot milk, whisking continuously over a low heat until the sauce thickens. Season and add a little nutmeg. Preheat the oven to Gas Mark 5/190°C/fan oven 170°C.

6 Pour the vegetable sauce into a 1.2 litre (2 pint) ovenproof dish and lay the aubergines on top. Pour over the onion and chive sauce and sprinkle the top with the grated cheese. Bake in the oven for 30 minutes until bubbling and golden. Spoon on to four plates and serve.

Vegetable pie

Serves 4

320 calories per serving

Takes 25 minutes to prepare,
  35 minutes to cook

Ⓥ

❄

350 g (12 oz) baby new
  potatoes, scrubbed and
  halved

175 g (6 oz) baby carrots,
  scrubbed and trimmed

225 g (8 oz) shelled broad
  beans

2 leeks, sliced

100 g (3½ oz) frozen peas

400 g can chopped tomatoes

1 tablespoon dried mixed
  herbs

2 tablespoons vermouth

8 x 45 g (1½ oz) sheets filo
  pastry, measuring
  50 x 24 cm (20 x 9½ inches)

25 g (1 oz) low fat spread,
  melted

salt and freshly ground black
  pepper

*This is a perfect dish for late spring and early summer,
when new potatoes and broad beans are at their best.*

1 Bring a pan of water to the boil, add the potatoes and carrots
and cook for 10 minutes. Add the beans, leeks and peas to the
pan and cook for a further 5 minutes.

2 Drain the vegetables and toss with the tomatoes, herbs and
vermouth. Season and spoon into an ovenproof dish.

3 Preheat the oven to Gas Mark 6/200°C/fan oven 180°C.

4 Keeping the filo pastry sheets together, brush the top sheet
with the low fat spread on one side and then crumple it up.
Repeat with all 8 sheets and then arrange the crumpled sheets
over the vegetables. Bake for 20 minutes, until the pastry is
crisp and golden. Serve hot.

Tip... Filo pastry is a useful standby to have in the freezer;
it turns simple food into something special.

Fajita-style stack

Serves 4

321 calories per serving

Takes 15 minutes to prepare,
15–20 minutes to cook

Ⓥ

This delicious twist on the classic Tex Mex dish can be made up to a day in advance and stored in the fridge. Serve with a herb salad, 1 tablespoon of reduced fat soured cream and ¼ x 170 g pot of reduced fat guacamole per person.

calorie controlled cooking spray

1 leek, sliced finely

350 g packet Quorn Chicken Style Pieces

1 red pepper, de-seeded and diced finely

30 g sachet fajita spice mix

2 tablespoons tomato purée

150 ml (5 fl oz) vegetable stock

4 x 50 g (1¾ oz) soft flour tortillas

150 g (5½ oz) low fat soft cheese with garlic and herbs

30 g (1¼ oz) half fat mature Cheddar cheese

1 Preheat the oven to Gas Mark 5/190°C/fan oven 170°C. Heat a non stick frying pan and spray with the cooking spray. Cook the leek, Quorn and pepper for 5 minutes. Add the fajita spices and tomato purée and cook for 1 minute, stirring. Pour in the stock and remove from the heat. Stir until the sauce comes together.

2 Spread a tortilla with a quarter of the soft cheese and put in the base of an 18 cm (7 inch), loose-bottomed, round cake tin. Top with a third of the Quorn mixture and continue the layers until everything is used up. Scatter over the cheese and bake in the oven for 15–20 minutes until golden. Remove from the cake tin and cut into wedges. Serve immediately.

Variation... For a non-vegetarian version, replace the Quorn with 400 g (14 oz) lean minced pork and cook with the leek and peppers in step 1.

Lasagne verde

Serves 4
580 calories per serving
Takes 40 minutes to prepare, 30 minutes to cook ❶ ❄

A lovely twist on traditional lasagne.

250 g (9 oz) no-precook lasagne sheets,
  preferably spinach

For the filling
1 round lettuce, shredded
450 g (1 lb) frozen peas
125 ml (4 fl oz) vegetable stock
calorie controlled cooking spray
2 garlic cloves, chopped finely
225 g (8 oz) courgettes, diced finely
125 ml (4 fl oz) white wine
a small bunch of fresh mint, chopped

500 g (1 lb 2 oz) frozen spinach, defrosted
200 g (7 oz) Quark
a pinch of grated nutmeg
salt and freshly ground black pepper

For the topping
2 eggs
4 tablespoons skimmed milk
300 g (10½ oz) low fat natural yogurt
100 g (3½ oz) low fat soft cheese
50 g (1¾ oz) half fat mature Cheddar cheese,
  grated

1 Place the lettuce, peas and stock in a lidded pan and cook, covered, for 20 minutes over a low heat.

2 Meanwhile, heat a large non stick frying pan and spray with the cooking spray. Sauté the garlic for 2 minutes and then add the courgettes. Stir-fry for 4 minutes over a high heat until the courgettes brown slightly. Add the wine and boil rapidly until all but a few tablespoons evaporate. Add the mint, toss and remove from the heat.

continues overleaf ▶

3 In another pan, gently heat the spinach and Quark. Add the nutmeg and seasoning.

4 Preheat the oven to Gas Mark 6/200°C/fan oven 180°C. Spray a 30 cm (12 inch) ovenproof dish with the cooking spray and line the bottom with lasagne sheets. Mix the cooked lettuce and peas together with the courgette and spinach mixtures and cover the pasta with a layer of vegetables in their juices. Top with lasagne and repeat twice more. Finish with a layer of pasta.

5 Beat together all the topping ingredients except the Cheddar cheese. Pour over the lasagne. Sprinkle with the cheese and bake for 30 minutes until golden.

Creamy mushroom tagliatelle

Serves 4
350 calories per serving
Takes 20 minutes
Ⓥ

350 g (12 oz) dried tagliatelle
calorie controlled cooking
  spray
2 garlic cloves, chopped
450 g (1 lb) mushrooms, sliced
juice of ½ a lemon
4 tablespoons virtually fat free
  plain fromage frais
salt and freshly ground black
  pepper
a small bunch of fresh chives,
  chopped finely, to garnish
  (optional)

A very quick, easy and satisfying pasta dish with only a few ingredients.

1 Bring a pan of water to the boil, add the pasta and cook according to the packet instructions.

2 Meanwhile, heat a large non stick frying pan, spray with the cooking spray and fry the garlic for 1 minute, until turning golden.

3 Add the mushrooms, season and stir-fry on a high heat for 4 minutes until they are soft and have absorbed all their juices. Add the lemon juice and cook for a further minute and then turn off the heat and stir in the fromage frais.

4 Drain the pasta, reserving a few tablespoons of the cooking liquid, toss in the sauce and check the seasoning. Serve garnished with the chives, if using.

Tip... When making pasta sauces, always try to reserve a few tablespoons of the pasta cooking liquid to add to the sauce. It improves the sauce's texture and helps it to bind to the pasta.

Aubergine cannelloni

Serves 4

259 calories per serving

Takes 35 minutes to prepare,
35 minutes to cook

Ⓥ

❄ (after step 4)

100 g (3½ oz) dried long grain
rice

2 large aubergines

calorie controlled cooking
spray

250 g (9 oz) cottage cheese
with onion and chives

a small bunch of fresh parsley,
chopped

400 g can chopped tomatoes
with herbs

1 onion, chopped finely

2 garlic cloves, chopped finely

a small bunch of fresh basil,
larger leaves torn

100 g (3½ oz) half fat Cheddar
cheese, grated

salt and freshly ground black
pepper

*There is no pasta in this 'cannelloni' recipe; slices of
grilled aubergine are used as a tasty alternative.*

1 Bring a pan of water to the boil, add the rice and cook
according to the packet instructions.

2 Meanwhile, preheat the grill to high and slice the aubergines
into thin slices lengthways. Season and spray with the cooking
spray. Grill for 5 minutes on one side and then turn and grill for
2 minutes more, until golden.

3 Preheat the oven to Gas Mark 4/180°C/fan oven 160°C.
Drain the rice and place in a large bowl with the cottage
cheese, parsley, seasoning and half the tomatoes. Mix
together.

4 Spray a non stick frying pan with the cooking spray and fry
the onion and garlic for 5 minutes, adding a splash of water if
necessary to prevent them from sticking. Add the rest of the
tomatoes and bring to the boil. Simmer for 5 minutes, season
and add the basil.

5 Place 2–3 tablespoons of the cottage cheese mixture on
each aubergine strip and roll up into a cylinder. Place in one
layer in an ovenproof lasagne dish and pour over the tomato
and basil sauce. Scatter with the Cheddar cheese and bake
for 35 minutes, until the cheese is golden and bubbling. Allow
to stand for a few minutes before serving.

Vegetable pasta bake

Serves 4

300 calories per serving

Takes 20 minutes to prepare,
30 minutes to cook

Ⓥ

700 g jar passata

calorie controlled cooking spray

300 g (10½ oz) carrots, peeled and diced

300 g (10½ oz) leeks, halved and sliced

500 g (1 lb 2 oz) courgettes, diced

2 garlic cloves, crushed

80 g (3 oz) mozzarella light, grated

8 fresh lasagne sheets

2 tablespoons half fat crème fraîche

salt and freshly ground black pepper

A meal in one dish, this is sure to be a hit with the whole family.

1 Preheat the oven to Gas Mark 5/190°C/fan oven 170°C. Put a layer of passata in the bottom of an ovenproof dish.

2 Heat a non stick pan, spray with the cooking spray and stir-fry the carrots for 6–8 minutes. Add the leeks and courgettes and cook for a further 2 minutes. The vegetables should be cooked but retain a little bite.

3 Meanwhile, in a small pan, heat the remaining passata, the garlic and half the cheese until the cheese melts and you have a smooth sauce. Season to taste.

4 To assemble the bake, mix the tomato sauce with the vegetables. Put three pasta sheets in the bottom of the dish and top with half the vegetable mixture. Cover with three more pasta sheets and then the remaining vegetables. Place the last two sheets in the middle of your dish, cover with the crème fraîche and then sprinkle the remaining cheese all over the top of the dish (not just over the pasta).

5 Bake in the preheated oven for 30 minutes.

Variations... Use the same amount of sliced mushrooms instead of courgettes.

You can use any dried pasta, cooking it for three-quarters of its cooking time before mixing in and baking.

Luxury cauliflower cheese

Serves 4
220 calories per serving
Takes 35 minutes
Ⓥ
❄

225 g (8 oz) leeks, sliced

175 g (6 oz) carrots, peeled and diced

450 g (1 lb) cauliflower, broken into florets

100 g (3½ oz) frozen peas

300 ml (10 fl oz) skimmed milk

200 g (7 oz) low fat soft cheese

25 g (1 oz) cornflour

25 g (1 oz) half fat Cheddar cheese, grated

15 g (½ oz) fresh wholemeal breadcrumbs

2 teaspoons olive oil

salt and freshly ground black pepper

Adding extra vegetables turns a simple cauliflower cheese into a tasty meal.

1 Bring a pan of water to the boil, add the leeks, carrots and cauliflower and cook for 5 minutes. Add the peas and cook for a further 5 minutes. Drain well.

2 Meanwhile, gently heat the milk and soft cheese together, whisking until smooth. Mix the cornflour with a little cold water to make a thin paste. When the milk and cheese mixture is almost boiling, add the cornflour paste and cook, stirring, until you have a thick and smooth sauce. Season to taste. Preheat the grill to medium.

3 Transfer the drained vegetables to a flameproof dish and pour over the sauce. Mix together the Cheddar cheese, breadcrumbs and olive oil and sprinkle over the top.

4 Grill for 2–3 minutes until the topping is bubbling and golden. Serve at once.

Portobello mushroom burgers

Serves 4
299 calories per serving
Takes 10 minutes to prepare,
20 minutes to cook
Ⓥ

1 heaped tablespoon chopped
  fresh thyme
1 garlic clove, crushed
finely grated zest and juice of
  ½ a lemon
4 extra large portobello or flat
  mushrooms
calorie controlled cooking
  spray
4 x 75 g (2¾ oz) ciabatta rolls
75 g (2¾ oz) reduced fat
  houmous
50 g (1¾ oz) 0% fat Greek
  yogurt
2 beef tomatoes, sliced
40 g (1½ oz) baby leaf salad
freshly ground black pepper

*The combination of herby baked mushrooms and houmous
is truly sublime as a light meal.*

1 Preheat the oven to Gas Mark 6/200°C/fan oven 180°C.
In a small bowl, mix the thyme, garlic, lemon zest and lemon
juice with black pepper and 1 tablespoon of water. Spray both
sides of the mushrooms with the cooking spray and place in
a non stick roasting tin, stalk side up. Drizzle on the herb and
lemon mixture and then cover the roasting tin with foil.

2 Put the roasting tin with the mushrooms in the oven, along
with the rolls placed on top of the foil to warm through, for
10 minutes. Remove the rolls. Take the foil off the mushrooms
and cook for a further 10 minutes.

3 Meanwhile, mix the houmous and yogurt together with a
seasoning of black pepper.

4 Split the rolls open and spread with the houmous mixture.
Add a few slices of tomato and a cooked mushroom to each
one, plus a small handful of salad leaves. Serve immediately.

Cannellini bean and courgette patties

Serves 4
149 calories per serving
Takes 30 minutes
◐
❄ (patties only)

**calorie controlled cooking
    spray**
2 courgettes, grated coarsely
**a bunch of spring onions,
    chopped**
2 garlic cloves, crushed
**1 tablespoon chopped fresh
    lemon thyme**
**2 x 410 g cans cannellini
    beans, drained and rinsed**
1 egg white, beaten lightly
**25 g (1 oz) grated Parmesan
    cheese**
freshly ground black pepper

To serve
75 g (2¾ oz) wild rocket
4 tomatoes, chopped roughly
4 teaspoons balsamic vinegar

*Enjoy this summery tasting combination of courgettes and
beans served with a fresh, light salad.*

1 Heat a non stick frying pan until hot and spray with the
cooking spray. Squeeze the excess liquid from the courgettes,
add to the pan and stir-fry with the spring onions, garlic and
lemon thyme for 4–5 minutes until wilted and soft.

2 Meanwhile, put the beans, egg white and Parmesan cheese
in a food processor and whizz to a purée. Add the courgette
mixture, season with black pepper and mix briefly. Using wet
hands, shape into 12 patties.

3 Wipe out the frying pan with kitchen towel and spray again
with the cooking spray. Cook the patties in two batches, for
2½ minutes on each side or until golden and hot.

4 Toss the rocket and tomatoes with the balsamic vinegar
and divide between four plates. Serve three patties per
person with the salad.

Tip... The patties can be made in advance and kept,
covered, in the fridge until ready to cook. If you are
planning to freeze the patties, do this before cooking. To
keep the individual patties separate when freezing, place
on a baking tray in a single layer, cover with cling film and
freeze until firm. Transfer to a plastic freezer bag and label
clearly.

Mediterranean macaroni cheese

Serves 4

360 calories per serving

Takes 20 minutes to prepare,
20 minutes to cook

Ⓥ

❄

425 ml (15 fl oz) skimmed milk
25 g (1 oz) cornflour
1 teaspoon English mustard
**100 g (3½ oz) half fat Red
Leicester cheese, grated**
**225 g (8 oz) dried quick cook
macaroni**
**50 g (1¾ oz) stoned black
olives in brine, drained and
halved**
2 tablespoons torn fresh basil
2 beefsteak tomatoes, sliced
**salt and freshly ground black
pepper**

*Adding basil, olives and sliced tomatoes makes the world
of difference to this popular dish.*

1 Reserve 3 tablespoons of milk and heat the rest, until
just boiling. In a bowl, mix the cornflour to a paste with the
reserved milk. Pour the hot milk into the cornflour paste and
stir well. Return the mixture to a clean pan and cook, stirring,
until the sauce thickens. Add the mustard and cheese and
stir until the cheese melts. Season to taste.

2 Bring a pan of water to the boil, add the pasta and cook for
about 5 minutes or according to the packet instructions. Drain
well and mix into the cheese sauce along with the halved olives
and basil.

3 Preheat the oven to Gas Mark 5/190°C/fan oven 170°C.
Spoon the macaroni mixture into an ovenproof dish and
arrange the tomato slices on top. Season with black pepper.
Bake in the oven for 20 minutes until bubbling. Serve hot.

Spring vegetable risotto

Serves 4
363 calories per serving
Takes 40 minutes
Ⓥ

225 g (8 oz) baby carrots, scrubbed and trimmed of all but a little of the tender tops

225 g (8 oz) baby turnips, scrubbed and trimmed of all but a little of their tops, quartered

225 g (8 oz) baby courgettes, sliced into thirds diagonally

calorie controlled cooking spray

1 garlic clove, chopped finely

1 onion, chopped finely

300 g (10½ oz) dried risotto rice

100 ml (3½ fl oz) dry white wine

1 litre (1¾ pints) hot vegetable stock

a small bunch of fresh parsley, chopped

salt and freshly ground black pepper

20 g (¾ oz) grated Parmesan cheese, to serve

a few fresh parsley sprigs, to garnish

A delicious, creamy risotto.

1 Bring a pan of water to the boil and steam the spring vegetables for 2–3 minutes, so they are still a little undercooked. Refresh them under cold water to stop them from cooking any more and then drain.

2 Meanwhile, heat a large non stick frying pan and spray with the cooking spray. Stir-fry the garlic and onion for 5 minutes, until softened and golden, adding a splash of water if necessary to prevent them from sticking. Add the rice and mix together.

3 Turn the heat to high, pour in the wine and stir-fry for a further 2 minutes, until all the wine has been absorbed.

4 Turn the heat down to medium, add a ladleful of hot stock, just to cover the rice and cook, stirring, until it is all absorbed. Continue adding one ladleful of stock at a time, following the same method, until all the stock has been absorbed.

5 The rice should now be tender but still slightly firm to the bite. Gently fold in the steamed drained vegetables and the parsley. Check the seasoning and serve sprinkled with the Parmesan cheese. Garnish with the parsley sprigs.

Veggie sausage ragu

Serves 4
479 calories per serving
Takes 35 minutes
☉
❄ (ragu sauce only)

350 g (12 oz) dried pasta shells
calorie controlled cooking spray
1 onion, diced finely
250 g packet vegetarian sausages, chopped
125 ml (4 fl oz) red wine
2 tablespoons tomato purée
300 ml (10 fl oz) vegetable stock
150 g (5½ oz) cherry tomatoes, halved
75 g (2¾ oz) roasted red peppers in brine, drained, de-seeded and diced
freshly ground black pepper

To serve
a generous handful of fresh basil leaves
50 g (1¾ oz) Parmesan cheese, grated

This is a great vegetarian version of a classic Italian sauce.

1 Bring a large pan of water to the boil, add the pasta and cook for 10 minutes, or according to the packet instructions, until al dente.

2 Meanwhile, heat a non stick saucepan and spray with the cooking spray. Cook the onion for 3–4 minutes until softened but not coloured. Spray the pan again with the cooking spray and add the sausages. Continue to cook for 5 minutes until starting to brown, stirring occasionally.

3 Add the wine to the sausage mix and bubble for 2 minutes, until reduced. Stir in the tomato purée and stock and gently simmer for 10 minutes.

4 Stir the tomatoes into the pan with the peppers and gently cook for 5 minutes until the tomatoes are beginning to soften. Season with black pepper.

5 Drain the pasta and return to the pan. Pour the sausage ragu into the pasta and stir to coat. Put into warmed bowls, scatter over the basil and top with the Parmesan.

Delicious desserts

Black Forest trifle

Serves 4

264 calories per serving

Takes 20 minutes +
10 minutes cooling

ⓨ

500 g bag frozen Black Forest fruits

1 tablespoon caster sugar

1 mulled wine spice bag

2 teaspoons cornflour

4 Weight Watchers Belgian Chocolate Slices, each cut into 9 cubes

125 ml (4 fl oz) half fat crème fraîche

30 g (1¼ oz) chilled plain chocolate (minimum 70% cocoa solids)

A classic that everyone will love.

1 Put half the Black Forest fruits into a bowl and set aside. Put the remaining fruits into a small saucepan with 100 ml (3½ fl oz) of water, the sugar and mulled wine spice bag. Bring to the boil and rapidly boil for 5 minutes. Pass through a sieve into a jug, pressing the fruit with the back of a spoon to squeeze out all the juice. (You should have about 200 ml/ 7 fl oz juice). Discard the fruit and spice bag.

2 Mix the cornflour to a paste with 1 tablespoon of water. Return the fruit juice to a small saucepan along with the dissolved cornflour. Bring to the boil and simmer for 1 minute, stirring until thickened. Pour this over the reserved frozen fruits in the bowl and leave to cool for 10 minutes.

3 Take four glasses and put three cubes of chocolate slices into each glass. Top each glass with a spoonful of the fruit and sauce and then a dollop of half fat crème fraîche. Continue layering until everything is used up. Grate the chocolate over each and serve.

Strawberry tarts

Serves 4

175 calories per serving

Takes 30 minutes + cooling

Ⓥ

❄ (pastry base only)

calorie controlled cooking spray

125 g (4½ oz) shortcrust pastry

1 tablespoon skimmed milk, for brushing

4 tablespoons Quark

2 heaped teaspoons icing sugar, plus extra for dusting

12 strawberries, hulled

A perfect summer dessert, these individual tarts have a creamy strawberry topping.

1 Preheat the oven to Gas Mark 6/200°C/fan oven 180°C. Spray a non stick baking tray with the cooking spray.

2 Roll the pastry out on baking parchment to 3 mm (⅛ inch) thick and cut out four 9 cm (3½ inch) rounds. Place on the baking tray and brush lightly with milk. Bake for 20 minutes until golden. Remove from the oven and leave to cool.

3 Meanwhile, in a bowl, mix together the Quark and icing sugar. Top the pastry rounds with a spoonful of the Quark mixture and stand three strawberries upright on each tart. Dust with a little icing sugar before serving.

Variation... In place of the strawberries, try 80 g (3 oz) raspberries or 2 peaches.

Rhubarb and custard jellies

Serves 4

45 calories per serving

Takes 10 minutes to prepare +
chilling, 20 minutes to cook

**350 g (12 oz) rhubarb, cut into
chunks**

**1 sachet raspberry or
strawberry sugar free jelly**

**2 tablespoons artificial
sweetener**

**150 g (5½ oz) ready-made low
fat custard**

A very simple pudding.

1 Place the rhubarb in a saucepan with 300 ml (10 fl oz) of
water. Bring to the boil, cover and simmer for 15 minutes until
tender. Stir in the jelly, mixing well and simmer for a further
2 minutes.

2 Remove from the heat and whisk in the artificial sweetener
and custard.

3 Divide between four individual serving dishes. Cool and then
chill until set.

Crema Italiana

Serves 4

173 calories per serving

Takes 25 minutes to prepare + chilling, 50 minutes to cook

ⓥ

50 g (1¾ oz) caster sugar
a kettleful of boiling water

For the coffee custard

3 eggs
50 g (1¾ oz) caster sugar
225 ml (8 fl oz) skimmed milk
5 tablespoons freshly brewed strong espresso coffee

1 Preheat the oven to Gas Mark 2/150°C/fan oven 130°C.

2 To make the caramel, put the sugar and 2 tablespoons of water in a saucepan. Heat over a low heat until all the sugar has dissolved, stirring occasionally and not allowing the mixture to boil. Once dissolved, turn up the heat and bring to a fast boil. Cook for about 10 minutes, swirling the pan occasionally, until the sugar is a dark golden colour – be brave and allow the caramel to darken without burning. Remove from the heat. Carefully and immediately, divide the mixture between four 150 ml (5 fl oz) ovenproof ramekins or mini pudding basins. Set aside.

3 To make the coffee custard, beat the eggs and sugar together in a mixing bowl. Gradually add the milk and then the coffee, whisking well. Pour the mixture through a sieve into a jug and then divide between the ramekins.

4 Transfer the ramekins to a shallow roasting tin. Pour boiling water into the tin to come no more than halfway up the sides of the dishes. Transfer the tin to the middle shelf of the oven and bake for 50 minutes until set but still a little wobbly.

5 Carefully remove from the oven and allow the water to cool slightly. Remove the ramekins from the water bath and leave until cold, Transfer to the refrigerator for at least 4 hours or preferably overnight.

6 To serve, run a sharp knife round the edge of each pudding and turn each out on to a serving plate, holding the two together. Shake sharply. You should hear the pudding release from the ramekin. Carefully remove to reveal the caramel sauce and serve immediately.

Blueberry crumbles

Serves 4

221 calories per serving

Takes 5 minutes to prepare,
20 minutes to cook

Ⓥ

**350 g (12 oz) frozen
blueberries**

1 tablespoon cornflour

**60 g (2 oz) light brown soft
sugar**

75 g (2¾ oz) plain white flour

40 g (1½ oz) low fat spread

25 g (1 oz) porridge oats

Little individual crumbles are fun for all the family.

1 Preheat the oven to Gas Mark 5/190°C/fan oven 170°C.

2 In a bowl, toss the blueberries together with the cornflour and 25 g (1 oz) of the sugar. Divide between four small ovenproof dishes or ramekins and add 1 tablespoon of water to each dish.

3 In a separate bowl, sift the flour and rub in the low fat spread until the mixture looks like breadcrumbs. Stir in the remaining sugar and the oats and then press the crumble mixture on top of the blueberries.

4 Place the dishes on a baking tray and bake in the oven for 20 minutes until the crumbles are golden and crisp and the blueberry juices are bubbling up from underneath.

Sticky toffee pudding

Serves 4

320 calories per serving

Takes 20 minutes to prepare,
40 minutes to cook

Ⓥ

❄

**calorie controlled cooking
spray**
50 g (1¾ oz) low fat spread
**50 g (1¾ oz) dark brown soft
sugar**
2 eggs, beaten
**100 g (3½ oz) self raising
white flour**
2 tablespoons boiling water
3 tablespoons golden syrup

*For all those with a sweet tooth, this is the pudding for you.
Serve with 3 tablespoons of ready-made low fat custard
per person.*

1 Spray four individual metal pudding moulds with a little
cooking spray.

2 Place the low fat spread and sugar in a warmed mixing bowl
and beat them together until fluffy. Beat in the eggs and then
fold in the flour with the boiling water.

3 Divide the golden syrup between the four moulds and then
spoon the sponge mixture over the top.

4 Transfer the moulds to a steamer and steam for 40 minutes.
Take care never to allow the steamer to boil dry, topping up
with boiling water if necessary.

5 To serve, carefully run a round bladed knife around the
edge of the moulds and turn them out on to four small serving
plates.

Tip... If you don't own a steamer, simply place an upturned
saucer in the base of a medium saucepan and add the
moulds. Pour a little water around the moulds and then
place the pan, covered, on the hob and steam for the same
time.

Baked bananas

Serves 4

168 calories per serving

Takes 25 minutes

Ⓥ

4 ripe bananas, unpeeled

40 g (1½ oz) plain chocolate (minimum 70% cocoa solids), broken into chunks

This dessert tastes absolutely delicious and is remarkably easy to make. If you like, serve with 60 g (2 oz) low fat ice cream per person.

1 Preheat the oven to Gas Mark 4/180°C/fan oven 160°C. Take a small knife and make a slit through the skin along the inner curve of each banana. Don't go all the way to the ends. Open out the cut slightly.

2 Divide the chocolate between the four bananas, pressing it into the slits. Wrap each banana in foil and place on a baking tray.

3 Bake in the oven for about 18–20 minutes or until the chocolate has melted. Serve a banana each.

Lemon meringue bake

Serves 4
237 calories per serving
Takes 23 minutes
ⓥ

4 x 24 g (1 oz) trifle sponges
60 g (2 oz) caster sugar
grated zest and juice of
  2 large lemons
2 tablespoons cornflour
2 egg whites
75 g (2¾ oz) icing sugar,
  sieved

Tangy lemon sauce soaks into trifle sponges, which are then topped with gooey meringue. If you like it really tart, add another lemon.

1 Preheat the oven to Gas Mark 6/200°C/fan oven 180°C. Arrange the trifle sponges in the bottom of a 1.2 litre (2 pint) ovenproof dish. Put 300 ml (10 fl oz) of cold water, the sugar, lemon zest and lemon juice in a saucepan and heat gently until the sugar has dissolved, stirring occasionally.

2 Meanwhile, mix the cornflour with 3 tablespoons of cold water until it forms a paste. Stir the paste into the lemon mixture, bring to the boil and cook for 1 minute until thickened. Pour the lemon sauce over the sponges and set aside.

3 In a clean, grease-free bowl, whisk the egg whites until they form stiff peaks. Put the bowl over a pan of barely simmering water and continue whisking, gradually adding the icing sugar until thick and glossy.

4 Spoon the meringue over the lemon sauce, using the back of a spoon to create swirls. Bake in the oven for 7–8 minutes until lightly golden.

Chocolate bread pudding with luscious chocolate sauce

Serves 4

242 calories per serving

Takes 20 minutes to prepare + chilling, 35–40 minutes to cook ⓥ

A rich, luxurious pudding that everyone will love.

½ teaspoon low fat spread

6 slices Weight Watchers Danish sliced white bread, crusts removed and cut into squares

600 ml (20 fl oz) skimmed milk

2 tablespoons unsweetened cocoa powder

2 eggs

25 g (1 oz) dark or light muscovado sugar

1 teaspoon vanilla essence

1 teaspoon icing sugar, for dusting

For the sauce

25 g (1 oz) plain chocolate (minimum 70% cocoa solids), broken into pieces

1 tablespoon unsweetened cocoa powder

150 ml (5 fl oz) skimmed milk

1 tablespoon cornflour

artificial sweetener, to taste

1 Grease a 20 cm (8 inch) square ovenproof dish with the low fat spread. Layer the bread squares in the dish.

2 In a small pan, gently heat the milk and cocoa powder together, stirring occasionally, until lukewarm.

3 In a bowl, whisk the eggs, sugar and vanilla essence together and then add the warm milk mixture and beat well. Strain into the baking dish, making sure that all the bread is covered. Cover and chill for 1–2 hours.

4 Preheat the oven to Gas Mark 4/180°C/fan oven 160°C. Bake the pudding for about 35–40 minutes or until set. Remove from the oven and set aside for 5 minutes.

5 While the pudding is cooling, make the sauce. Put the chocolate, cocoa powder, milk and cornflour in a saucepan and heat gently, stirring until smooth and blended. Add sweetener to taste. Dust the pudding with the icing sugar and serve with the hot sauce.

Quick baked apples with plums and sultanas

Serves 4

130 calories per serving

Takes 15 minutes to prepare,
  6–8 minutes to cook

Ⓥ

4 cooking apples, peeled and
  cored

6 plums, stoned and sliced

1 heaped tablespoon sultanas

artificial sweetener, to taste

4 heaped tablespoons reduced
  sugar strawberry jam

This easy dessert will satisfy everyone's sweet tooth. For a real treat, serve with 75 g (2¾ oz) ready-made low fat custard per person.

1 Put the cooking apples in a microwaveable dish. Mix the plums with the sultanas and use this mixture to fill the cavities in the apples.

2 Sprinkle the apples with artificial sweetener and then place a heaped tablespoon of strawberry jam on top of each one.

3 Cook in the microwave on high for 6–8 minutes, or until the apples are tender and the jam has melted.

4 Serve the apples with the hot syrupy mixture spooned over and around them.

Tip... You can also cook these in the oven at Gas Mark 4/ 180°C/fan oven 160°C for 40 minutes.

Very berry ice

Serves 4

88 calories per serving

Takes 15 minutes + 3½ hours
  freezing + softening
❄

**12 g sachet sugar free
  raspberry jelly**

300 ml (10 fl oz) boiling water

**350 g (12 oz) mixed summer
  berries, e.g. raspberries,
  strawberries, blackcurrants**

**200 g (7 oz) low fat vanilla
  yogurt**

*If you want to make this recipe even easier, once the
yogurt has been mixed in, skip the whisking of the frozen
mixture, pour it into eight lolly moulds and then freeze until
firm. Dip the moulds into hot water to release the lollies.*

1 In a measuring jug, sprinkle the jelly crystals over the boiling
water and stir to dissolve. Make the mixture up to 600 ml
(20 fl oz) with cold water.

2 Using a blender or hand blender, whizz the fruits to a purée
and then mix with the jelly. Pour into a shallow tray or plastic
box, cover and place in the freezer for 1½ hours, until beginning
to freeze around the edges. Whisk the mixture, making sure that
you mix in the frozen bits from around the edge of the container.
Mix in the vanilla yogurt until smooth and then return the mixture
to the freezer.

3 Whisk the mixture twice more, at intervals of roughly 1 hour.
The whisking process breaks up large ice crystals, so that you
get a smoother textured ice.

4 Once the ice is firm, serve in scoops. If the ice has been left
to freeze completely solid, it will need to soften in the fridge
for 30 minutes or so before scooping, or it can be softened on
defrost in the microwave, in blasts of 30 seconds, until ready.

Slow-baked saffron rice pudding

Serves 4

120 calories per serving

Takes 30 minutes to prepare,
 1¼ hours to cook

Ⓥ

8 saffron strands
600 ml (20 fl oz) skimmed milk
25 g (1 oz) caster sugar
a pinch of grated nutmeg
**50 g (1¾ oz) dried pudding
 rice**

*Saffron gives this family favourite a glorious colour and
flavour.*

1 Place the saffron in a measuring jug. Heat the milk
until boiling and pour over the saffron. Leave to infuse for
20 minutes, stirring from time to time.

2 Preheat the oven to Gas Mark 3/170°C/fan oven 150°C. Mix
together the caster sugar, nutmeg and pudding rice and place
in a shallow ovenproof dish.

3 Pour the milk over the rice, stir well and bake for 1¼ hours,
stirring halfway through cooking.

Variation... Other flavourings you can use instead of saffron
include lemon zest and cinnamon or a few drops of almond
or vanilla essence.

Pear brûlées

Serves 4
130 calories per serving
Takes 15 minutes
Ⓥ

1 large ripe pear (e.g. Comice, Conference), chopped
200 g (7 oz) Quark
140 g (5 oz) low fat lemon or vanilla yogurt
4 tablespoons demerara sugar

These fruit brûlées are a healthy version of a favourite dessert.

1 Preheat the grill to high. Divide the pear between four flameproof ramekins.

2 Beat together the Quark and yogurt until smooth and spoon the mixture on top of the pears. Sprinkle the tops evenly with the sugar.

3 Place the dishes under the hot grill to caramelise the sugar until it dissolves.

4 Allow the brûlées to cool for 5 minutes before serving.

Tip... If you have a cook's blow torch, you can flame the sugar with that.

Variation... All sorts of fruits could be used instead of pears. Try raspberries, sliced peaches, strawberries or plums.

Chocolate profiteroles

Serves 4

300 calories per serving

Takes 25 minutes to prepare
 + cooling, 15–20 minutes
 to cook

Ⓥ

25 g (1 oz) low fat spread

75 g (2¾ oz) plain white flour

1 egg

1 egg yolk

500 g (1 lb 2 oz) 0% fat Greek
 yogurt

2 teaspoons vanilla essence

1 tablespoon clear honey

2 tablespoons cornflour

2 tablespoons low fat drinking
 chocolate

300 ml (10 fl oz) skimmed milk

Discover these amazing profiteroles.

1 Preheat the oven to Gas Mark 6/200°C/fan oven 180°C and line a baking tray with non stick baking parchment.

2 Heat the low fat spread and 150 ml (5 fl oz) of water together in a large saucepan until the spread has just melted. Meanwhile put the flour on a piece of baking parchment.

3 Take the saucepan off the heat and, working quickly, add all the flour mix into the pan using the baking parchment as a funnel. Beat together with a wooden spoon for at least 1 minute until well blended and the mixture comes away from the side of the pan in one lump. Allow to cool for 10 minutes.

4 Beat together the whole egg and egg yolk and add to the cooled mixture, half at a time. Beat with a wooden spoon until the mixture is smooth, thick and glossy – this is quite hard.

5 Place 12 heaped teaspoons well apart on the baking tray and bake for 15–20 minutes until well risen and golden. Remove from the oven and, with a sharp knife, slit each profiterole to let the air out. Place back in the turned off oven, the door slightly ajar so they dry out inside and cool.

6 Mix together the yogurt, vanilla and honey. Spoon into the cool profiteroles and pile them up on a serving plate.

7 Blend the cornflour and drinking chocolate with a little of the milk in a saucepan. Blend in the rest of the milk and bring to the boil, stirring all the time, until thickened and smooth. Pour over the profiteroles to serve.

Index

A

apples, quick baked, with plums
and sultanas 164
apricot turnovers 22
aubergine cannelloni 134

B

bacon:
eggy crumpets 'n' bacon 14
minestrone soup 25
the ultimate hash browns 16
baked bananas 158
baked cheesy pots 28
bananas:
baked bananas 158
banana pancakes with maple
syrup 20
Basque chicken casserole 86
beans:
cannellini bean and courgette
patties 140
chilli con carne 50
beef:
chilli con carne 50
family beef cobbler 64
kebabs with mint and yogurt
dip 36
spaghetti bolognese 42
spicy meatballs 54
steak fajitas 62
biryani, chicken 72
Black Forest trifle 148
blueberry crumbles 156
bolognese, spaghetti 42

bread pudding, chocolate, with
luscious chocolate sauce 162
brûlées, pear 168
burgers:
portobello mushroom
burgers 138
tzatziki turkey burgers 74

C

cannellini bean and courgette
patties 140
cannelloni:
aubergine cannelloni 134
turkey cannelloni 92
casseroles:
Basque chicken casserole 86
sausage casserole 60
venison casserole 58
cauliflower cheese, luxury 137
cheese:
baked cheesy pots 28
cheese, onion and tomato
quiche 38
cheesy turkey meatloaf 70
luxury cauliflower cheese 137
Mediterranean macaroni
cheese 142
stuffed chicken breasts 90
chick peas:
creamy lamb korma 56
chicken:
Basque chicken casserole 86
chicken biryani 72
coriander chicken tikka 32
creamy chicken bake 76

lemon chicken 82
Monday's pie 79
Oriental chicken parcels 88
roast chicken with rosemary
and lemon potatoes 68
satay chicken 34
stuffed chicken breasts 90
Thai chicken curry 78
chilli con carne 50
chocolate:
baked bananas 158
Black Forest trifle 148
chocolate bread pudding with
luscious chocolate sauce
162
chocolate profiteroles 170
chorizo pizza with warm potato
salad 53
chunky fish fingers 98
cobbler, family beef 64
cod:
chunky fish fingers 98
cod and leek parcels 114
fish and chips 96
Italian fish stew 110
roasted tomato cod with parsley
mash 118
traditional fishcakes 105
coriander chicken tikka 32
courgette patties, cannellini bean
and 140
crab:
spicy crab cakes 35
Thai noodles with crab
meat 116

crema Italiana 154
creamy chicken bake 76
creamy lamb korma 56
creamy mushroom tagliatelle 133
creamy pesto pasta 80
crumbles, blueberry 156
crumpets 'n' bacon, eggy 14
curries:
   chicken biryani 72
   coriander chicken tikka 32
   creamy lamb korma 56
   one pot veggie curry 122
   smoked haddock kedgeree 18
   Thai chicken curry 78
custard jellies, rhubarb and 152

D
dip, mint and yogurt, kebabs
   with 36

E
eggs:
   baked cheesy pots 28
   eggy crumpets 'n' bacon 14
   oven-baked tomatoes and
      eggs 24
   the ultimate hash browns 16

F
fajitas:
   fajita-style stack 128
   steak fajitas 62
family beef cobbler 64
fish:
   chunky fish fingers 98
   cod and leek parcels 114
   fish and chips 96
   fish pie 108

Italian fish stew 110
pizza marinara 100
roasted tomato cod with parsley
   mash 118
salmon steaks in foil 115
smoked haddock kedgeree 18
traditional fishcakes 105
tuna and sweetcorn rosti
   cake 102
tuna pasta Niçoise 30
fresh pea and ham pasta 61
fruit:
   apricot turnovers 22
   baked bananas 158
   banana pancakes with maple
      syrup 20
   Black Forest trifle 148
   blueberry crumbles 156
   lemon meringue bake 160
   pear brûlées 168
   quick baked apples with plums
      and sultanas 164
   rhubarb and custard jellies 152
   roast lamb with fruity herb
      stuffing 52
   strawberry tarts 150
   very berry ice 166

H
haddock:
   fish pie 108
   smoked haddock kedgeree 18
ham:
   baked cheesy pots 28
   fresh pea and ham pasta 61
   stuffed chicken breasts 90
hash browns, the ultimate 16

I
ice, very berry 166
Italian fish stew 110

J
jellies, rhubarb and custard 152

K
kebabs with mint and yogurt
   dip 36
kedgeree, smoked haddock 18
korma, creamy lamb 56

L
lamb:
   creamy lamb korma 56
   roast lamb with fruity herb
      stuffing 52
   shepherd's pie 46
lasagne verde 130
leek parcels, cod and 114
lemon:
   lemon chicken 82
   lemon meringue bake 160
   roast chicken with rosemary
      and lemon potatoes 68
lentils:
   one pot veggie curry 122
   vegetable and lentil
      moussaka 124
luxury cauliflower cheese 137

M
macaroni cheese,
   Mediterranean 142
meatballs, spicy 54
meatloaf, cheesy turkey 70

Mediterranean macaroni cheese 142
meringue bake, lemon 160
minestrone soup 25
mini toad in the hole 44
Monday's pie 79
moussaka, vegetable and lentil 124
mushrooms:
  creamy mushroom tagliatelle 133
  portobello mushroom burgers 138

N
noodles:
  prawn stir-fry 112
  sweet and sour pork noodles 48
  teriyaki turkey noodles 84
  Thai noodles with crab meat 116

O
one pot veggie curry 122
Oriental chicken parcels 88
oven-baked tomatoes and eggs 24

P
pancakes, banana, with maple syrup 20
pasta:
  creamy chicken bake 76
  creamy mushroom tagliatelle 133
  creamy pesto pasta 80
  fresh pea and ham pasta 61
  lasagne verde 130
  Mediterranean macaroni cheese 142
  minestrone soup 25
  spaghetti bolognese 42
  spicy seafood and tomato pasta 106
  tuna pasta Niçoise 30
  turkey cannelloni 92
  vegetable pasta bake 136
  veggie sausage ragu 144
pastry:
  apricot turnovers 22
  cheese, onion and tomato quiche 38
  Monday's pie 79
  seafood and parsley tart 104
  strawberry tarts 150
  vegetable pie 127
patties, cannellini bean and courgette 140
pea and ham pasta, fresh 61
pear brûlées 168
pies:
  fish pie 108
  Monday's pie 79
  shepherd's pie 46
  vegetable pie 127
pizza:
  chorizo pizza with warm potato salad 53
  pizza marinara 100
plums and sultanas, quick baked apples with 164
pork:
  mini toad in the hole 44
  sausage casserole 60
  sweet and sour pork noodles 48
portobello mushroom burgers 138

potatoes:
  chorizo pizza with warm potato salad 53
  fish and chips 96
  fish pie 108
  oven-baked tomatoes and eggs 24
  roast chicken with rosemary and lemon potatoes 68
  roasted tomato cod with parsley mash 118
  shepherd's pie 46
  spicy crab cakes 35
  the ultimate hash browns 16
  traditional fishcakes 105
  tuna and sweetcorn rosti cake 102
prawns:
  fish pie 108
  Italian fish stew 110
  pizza marinara 100
  prawn stir-fry 112
profiteroles, chocolate 170

Q
quiche, cheese, onion and tomato 38
quick baked apples with plums and sultanas 164
quick tomato soup 26
Quorn:
  fajita-style stack 128

R
ragu, veggie sausage 144
rhubarb and custard jellies 152
rice:
  aubergine cannelloni 134

chicken biryani 72
lemon chicken 82
Oriental chicken parcels 88
slow-baked saffron rice
   pudding 167
smoked haddock kedgeree 18
spring vegetable risotto 143
risotto, spring vegetable 143
roast chicken with rosemary and
   lemon potatoes 68
roast lamb with fruity herb
   stuffing 52
roasted tomato cod with parsley
   mash 118
rosti cake, tuna and sweetcorn
   102

S
salads:
   chorizo pizza with warm potato
      salad 53
   tuna pasta Niçoise 30
salmon steaks in foil 115
satay chicken 34
sausages:
   mini toad in the hole 44
   sausage casserole 60
   veggie sausage ragu 144
seafood:
   fish pie 108
   Italian fish stew 110
   pizza marinara 100
   prawn stir-fry 112
   seafood and parsley tart 104
   spicy crab cakes 35
   spicy seafood and tomato
      pasta 106
   Thai noodles with crab
      meat 116

shepherd's pie 46
slow-baked saffron rice
   pudding 167
smoked haddock kedgeree 18
soup:
   minestrone soup 25
   quick tomato soup 26
spaghetti bolognese 42
spicy crab cakes 35
spicy meatballs 54
spicy seafood and tomato
   pasta 106
spring vegetable risotto 143
steak fajitas 62
stew, Italian fish 110
sticky toffee pudding 157
stuffed chicken breasts 90
stuffing, fruity herb, roast lamb
   with 52
strawberry tarts 150
sweet and sour pork noodles 48
sweetcorn rosti cake, tuna
   and 102

T
tarts:
   seafood and parsley tart 104
   strawberry tarts 150
teriyaki turkey noodles 84
Thai chicken curry 78
Thai noodles with crab meat 116
the ultimate hash browns 16
tikka, coriander chicken 32
toad in the hole, mini 44
tomatoes:
   cheese, onion and tomato
      quiche 38

oven-baked tomatoes and
   eggs 24
quick tomato soup 26
roasted tomato cod with parsley
   mash 118
spicy seafood and tomato
   pasta 106
tortillas:
   fajita-style stack 128
   steak fajitas 62
traditional fishcakes 105
trifle, Black Forest 148
tuna:
   pizza marinara 100
   tuna and sweetcorn rosti
      cake 102
   tuna pasta Niçoise 30
turkey:
   cheesy turkey meatloaf 70
   creamy pesto pasta 80
   teriyaki turkey noodles 84
   turkey cannelloni 92
   tzatziki turkey burgers 74
turnovers, apricot 22
tzatziki turkey burgers 74

V
vegetables:
   one pot veggie curry 122
   spring vegetable risotto 143
   vegetable and lentil
      moussaka 124
   vegetable pasta bake 136
   vegetable pie 127
veggie sausage ragu 144
venison casserole 58
very berry ice 166

Other titles in the Weight Watchers Mini Series

ISBN 978-0-85720-932-0

ISBN 978-0-85720-935-1

ISBN 978-0-85720-934-4

ISBN 978-0-85720-938-2

ISBN 978-0-85720-931-3

ISBN 978-0-85720-937-5

ISBN 978-0-85720-936-8

ISBN 978-0-85720-933-7

ISBN 978-1-47111-084-9

ISBN 978-1-47111-089-4

ISBN 978-1-47111-091-7

ISBN 978-1-47111-087-0

ISBN 978-1-47111-090-0

ISBN 978-1-47111-085-6

ISBN 978-1-47111-088-7

ISBN 978-1-47111-086-3

For more details please visit www.simonandschuster.co.uk